dress like a star

Vain trifles as they seem,
clothes change our view of the world
and the world's view of us.

Virginia Woolf

Annebelle van Tongeren

dress like a star

for every woman who wants to look her best

Aurum

First published in Great Britain 2008
by Aurum Press Ltd, 7 Greenland Street, London NW1 0ND
www.aurumpress.co.uk

Published by arrangement with Random House Australia.

A catalogue record for this book is available from the British Library.

ISBN 978 1 84513 395 5

10 9 8 7 6 5 4 3 2 1
2012 2011 2010 2009 2008

For more style tips, visit the author's website: www.yourwardrobemistress.com.au

Illustrations by Alex Wilson and Annebelle van Tongeren
Internal concept by Christabella Designs
Internal design by Warren Ventures
Printed in China

Dedication

For Stella and Valentina

Acknowledgements

I'm so grateful to Selwa Anthony for having faith in my manuscript and sending it to the amazing team at Random House. Thanks so much to Anna, Christa, Nikla, Vanessa and Sara who tailored it to look and sound gorgeous, and to Carmen, who whipped it into shape. Jumbo XXXL-sized thanks go to the extraordinary Jill Brown, who put so much effort into this book and supported me through the process. Thanks to Alex Wilson for her divine illustrations, created under great pressure. Biggest thanks of all to my bossy sister, Gaye, and my darling husband, Martyn, who nagged me to write it; to Jessica and Missy for their endless support; and to Valentina, who makes every day beautiful.

Contents

Once upon a time in a wardrobe on Planet Glamazon, far, far away, there was an outfit. It was a magic outfit made of the softest silk, spun by the most exotic silkworms in the galaxy. The stitches were so tiny that even the fairies who had sat up late sewing this wondrous creation could hardly see them. It was embellished with the most exotic and rare gemstones in the universe. Whoever wore this ensemble would be instantly stunning and command the hearts of the paparazzi, for this outfit was one-size-fits-all. It would would miraculously transform itself into the most flattering style for the would-be A-lister, intrinsically knowing what it needed to highlight and conceal, in order to be called The One.

After a particularly big night on Planet Glamazon, the Evil Empress of Doom found the outfit carelessly cast onto the floor by one of the Dancing Space Party Posse. The posse woke to see the empress trying to steal the ensemble and they all rushed to take it from her pointy, cold fingers. The most wondrous of outfits was shredded, torn between the Party Posse and the Evil Empress, who was laughing maniacally – as evil empresses do. The paparazzi took more photos than they could ever use.

And would-be A-listers all over the universe would forevermore search in vain for an outfit that would make them as fabulous as The One . . .

Introduction

Ladies . . .

Getting a decent outfit shouldn't have to be the stuff of myths and legends. However, I would like to start by making a blanket apology to all the people that I may offend over the next 212 pages. I have spent the past twenty years working as a television stylist, playing the role of wardrobe mistress and fairy godmother, actively trying to make each woman I dress stand out, look taller and thinner and separate from the rest of the crowd; to draw out her inner glamazon and make her feel like she is the most amazing woman in the room, or the most beautiful bride that walked down any aisle. Sadly, this drive to make my clients seem taller and thinner reinforces that tried and tested and politically corrected belief that in order to look gorgeous and be chock-full of confidence, you need to fit the fashion world's expectations and be born a leggy glamazon.

If I'm alarming you right now, put this book down immediately and go read *The Beauty Myth* instead. If you are tall and wafer thin, please buy whatever dress takes your fancy, because you're going to look great in anything. I'm serious.

Ideally, as the worlds of fashion, media and movies dictate, in order to be gorgeous you need to be young, 180 centimetres tall and a size 8. Oh, and you need perfect skin, glossy hair, straight teeth and whatever the handbag *du jour* is. As thoroughly modern women of the new millennium, we outwardly condemn this ridiculous expectation of our gender – but we still love our glossies and gossip mags, and secretly wish we were a lot more like Mischa Barton and a lot less like that woman in the supermarket queue three places in front of us with the very bad VPL and arms that are screaming to be exfoliated.

Okay, so maybe that's just my supermarket. And it's off my chest now. But if you share any of my feelings of being physically a bit of an underachiever, we can begin.

I come from a big family and, as daughter number five, was earmarked for the convent just like St Theresa, the Little Flower. For traditionally that is why God gives people fifth daughters. But I was more like Poison Ivy, and decided I really couldn't deal with the uniform and the severe haircuts. (The footwear was the true deal-breaker, though.) In our house we lived the concept 'First in, best dressed'. Yet among all the fashion conflicts with my sisters, I did listen to my mother and take on board a lot of the wise, penny-conscious Irish-Catholic principles that she instilled in her daughters, such as:

God gave us all talents.

In the Bible story, talents were a currency and the three characters in the parable were given unequal, and therefore unfair, amounts. But they all had to use them as best they could. Because that's all they got. The talents I refer to are somewhat shallower than the Bible's. We get judged, beauty-pageant style, on what we do with our *physical talents*. Some people get more – Mischa Barton, for example, has endless legs, modelesque height and a ridiculous level of general gorgeousness – and some people, possibly like you, and definitely like me, get less. That's just the way it is, so there is no point coveting thy neighbour's goat about it. We are what we are and it's high time we learned to invest our talents. And you know we are all answerable to the Big Guy if we dare waste them. Or get tattoos. (Actually, that's not in the Bible. It's just my opinion that God would see being tattooed as ruining his intellectual property with graffiti.)

What you can't disguise you emphasise.

I would like to add my own slant to this concept. What you can't eradicate, you need to disguise, and then emphasise something better. My theory is better than Mum's, but sadly the rhyming gets quite lost in my version.

It's what's on the inside that counts.

Yes, that's true with regard to wearing the correct underwear and making sure that your evening gown is properly supported with boning etc., but in my world I have changed the saying to: *It's what's on the outside that counts.* Really, it's true. If you are feeling confident about what you are wearing on the outside, you are going to feel 100 per cent better on the inside as you take on the challenges of your day. Or night.

You can look great no matter what your budget.

With nine children to bring up on a shoestring, somehow my mother always had us wearing the best, most current, quality clothes. And my sisters and I were six vain girls.

Mum knew the various body shapes and heights of her daughters well and was a home seamstress, like lots of the older women in our culture. Sadly, the days of 'nice young ladies' being expected to know how to sew seem to be gone and we have to rely on the choices available in stores. My four older sisters sang a lot and were forever going on television and entering competitions, so they needed a growing collection of amazing gowns in which to perform. Mum's patterns were adjusted here and there in lengths and in design lines to make the sisters all look the same. And they looked so beautiful as a gang of four. She would use embellishment or different fabrics to play up a feature, give more curves to the skinny one or conceal the dreaded 'Linane' legs that two inherited from her side of the family. Each dress was exactly right for the wearer and exactly right for the group as well. My mother is a fashion genius.

So how do we mere mortals with all our flaws seek out our own best outfits? Most people don't instinctively know what styles are right for them, and rely on everyone else to tell them. Feelings of physical inadequacy can leave us vulnerable to purchasing and blindly wearing whatever the Emperor's Latest New Clothes are deemed to be. But who is designing these clothes, and for whom? Guaranteed, they are designed for those same size 8, tall young glamazons I described earlier. They will look great on those girls. Definitely. But we mere mortals are stuck in the same place in the great circle of fashion paranoia and frustration. Having a fat/short/aged moment . . . and a KitKat while we work out what our story will be when we go back to the store and talk our way into getting a refund on the purchase.

Here is the most important thing I can tell anyone under thirty who has grown up in the celebrity-soaked culture we now live in. It needs to become a mantra:

Just because it looks great on Mischa Barton and people call it fabulous, doesn't mean that it will look any good on you.

Men seem to think we enjoy the torture of shopping. Of standing in change rooms mentally assaulting ourselves all day. Of credit-card bills that get so silly you can't open the mail any more. And of the ever-growing handbag collection. Have you noticed that the 'must have' signature bag changes faster than the length of the billing cycle of the lovely people at Visa? Have you experienced the blind panic of realising you are carrying a handbag that is at least three minutes out of date? That the £400 Christian Louboutin 'it' shoe all the mags told you to buy last month is now in the chain stores for less than £50, looks exactly the same as yours and is *wrong wrong wrong?* Or that dewy foundation changed to matte in the last edition of *Harper's Bazaar* and you didn't realise? The purchasing expectations imposed on us via the A-lister Party Posse are out of hand.

You see, what it comes down to is that most of us – shock, horror – are not glamazons and actresses. We all have great aspects to our figures (and some not-so-great ones as well). We can all find areas to celebrate in our bodies. Oh yes, we can. And we will highlight these.

You don't need to be tall. Think Kylie Minogue. Thumbelina. Shortest little popette you ever did see, but all her clothes are cut to her proportions.

You don't need to be young. Think Geena Davis and Julianne Moore, who wear their maturity so well.

Curves? Beyoncé would never be accused of having an eating disorder, and she looks great. So does Oprah. They know how to dress the sets of curves they own.

Short legs? We can work with that. It's about balance.

No bust? Not a problem.

Hips like a small planet? There are ways.

The idea is to minimise your less loved areas and play up your best features. But first you need to get really, really honest with yourself. And be prepared to be not necessarily mainstream.

You are the height you are, give or take a stiletto heel. Your shoulder line, your neck length, your leg length, your basic body shape – these define you physically. You can become a gym bunny, which will make you healthier and firmer, or get surgery to change certain areas, but your framing will stay basically unchanged. You can add a C cup or some killer abs, but the basic outline will remain.

I know that you are already well aware that some clothes just work on you. Inexplicably, a particular garment will make you look gorgeous, for what seems to be no apparent reason. It may seem like The One, but there is no magic involved. I'm here to tell you that there is a reason. A set of principles that make an outfit flatter *you*. Once you know what will work on your frame you will never feel overwhelmed or intimidated into buying an outfit you are unsure about again. (And there really is a sound reason that Roland Mouret's Galaxy dress sells for £1000.)

There are any number of stylists out there working in the media who will promote one label or another. They are employed to show us what is new and what is deemed to be fabulous. And we have some fantastic talent driving our fashion industry. But it needs to be said that what works in a magazine spread doesn't often work in real life. The thing to impress upon you is that just because a dress comes in your size, it doesn't mean it will make you look good. The gown designed for a sample size 10 is not made with a short size 14 in mind. It's made so that a short size 14 will buy into the dream of being a sample size 10 and open her wallet, then take it to the alteration lady and have 12 centimetres cut off the hem.

Don't buy something just because you can fit into it.

Slavishly following the direction of the stylists and fashion editors will not necessarily allow you to look like the best version of you that you can be. It is completely possible, though, to look through red carpet pages and paparazzi pics and choose contemporary pieces from the collections *that will flatter you*, if you know the parameters of which styles work on you.

It also needs to be said that if you cast an educated eye over the front row of any fashion-week parade, the fash pack are not practising what they preach. They specifically *don't* want to look like what they promote, because that would be a fashion faux pas worse than death. I have not seen the bobby-socks-and-chunky-heels look on a front-row fashion editor yet, and still they are tediously putting that combo in the mags. So please consider what the agenda is here. It's about the business of selling fashion, based on our insecurities.

The glossies can wax lyrical about which designer is flavour of the month and that's wonderful if you would like to be part of that scenario, supporting and strengthening our economy by making extra fashion purchases. (And thereby securing the employment of most of my friends.) But if you just want to look great, shop effectively and spend your cash with confidence, then read on.

Believe me when I say that the TV personalities I have dressed who you would least expect to have the same body issues and insecurities as you, definitely do have them. When I dress talent, especially for the very competitive area called the Red Carpet, there are principles and tricks of the trade that I use every time to make sure they look as good as they can, and you can use these, too. *Everybody is perfectly capable of scrubbing up a treat if they go about things logically.* And most celebrities look just as ordinary as you and me when they have their morning coffee. They get pimples and cold sores, they have bad hair days and they bloat at that time of the month as well. So relax.

I want you to know what is right for your body. To be able to go into a shop and know exactly what you are looking for. If it's a formal affair, to be able to spend your money wisely in a store, or visit a dressmaker with a design you will be certain will be worth the effort of making.

Dress Like a Star outlines the principles of determining what works on your specific body. It enables you to determine what kind of star you want to be, whether that's a Kidman, a Zeta-Jones, a Diaz, a Stefani or a Witherspoon – I'm talking classic Hollywood, elegant, gorgeous and impeccably dressed, and not a walking billboard for fashionable-for-a-minute labels or carving-out-a-look music stars. *Dress Like a Star* also clarifies the process of choosing eveningwear and bridal – some of the biggest fashion purchases you will make, and for which there will be everlasting photographic evidence of whether you got it wrong or followed these principles and got it oh so right.

A Star is Born

The basic body shapes

The first step to knowing how to choose the right clothes and accessories for your figure is to get an accurate idea of your body shape. There are six archetypal body shapes for women:

1 **Kate** is very thin.
2 **Elle** is broad through the shoulders.
3 **Beyoncé** is the classic curvaceous hourglass.
4 **Jennifer** is bootylicious.
5 **Liz**, bless her, is the glamazon shape we are constantly exposed to.
6 **Sheila** is the standard fashion industry sample.

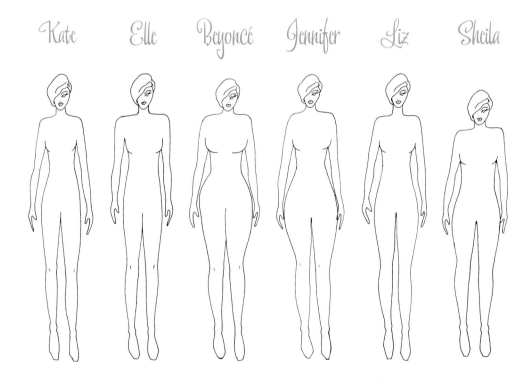

Kate   Elle   Beyoncé   Jennifer   Liz   Sheila

Sheila and Liz are only there for comparison and so you can always have it in mind that these are the two body types the fashion industry works around. The designs are done to look great in the marketing campaigns on Liz, and constructed to fit best on Sheila.

This is not intended to depress you, but a garment designed for Sheila, modelled by Liz, is probably not going to look very flattering on a short-waisted, lumpy-legged size 14 me or you.

It's not a matter of simply adjusting the shop's size 14 garment to be bigger or smaller in dimensions so that it fits. It's about working around the body that you have. *Your silhouette.*

Know your silhouette

To work out your own silhouette you're going to make what I like to call a 'paper doll' of yourself. Remember doing that when you were a kid? Well, this is a similar idea, only the adult version involves cameras and underwear . . . and not in a sleazy Hollywood Hills way.

Your paper doll will be a mini you, and you will use it to analyse your body shape and then, later on, to experiment with different outfits to find the ones that suit you best.

First, have a photograph taken of yourself. For this you should stand against a plain background wearing just your underwear. Chances are you haven't got the equipment to do this on your own, in which case perhaps you could ask your sister or trusted best friend to do it for you – even better, you could return the favour for her and you could work through this process together. (If you're not so keen on getting down to your underwear, a swimsuit would be fine, too, so long as it's not bulky and doesn't distort your outline.)

Make sure that you are standing straight with your feet slightly apart, looking at the camera, arms loosely by your side.

Get a print made of your photo, then lay a white piece of paper over the top and trace around your outline. Now cut it out, and you'll have your very own paper doll that shows clearly what silhouette you have. At this stage you only need one of these paper dolls, but it helps to make lots of them as they'll come in handy later, when it's time to plan your wardrobe.

Choose the silhouette archetype from the gallery on page 12 that is closest to your own so you can identify which star silhouette you are most like.

Remember, these celebrities have professionals on hand to guide them, so it is well worth looking through pictures of their best outfits to get an idea of what shapes actually work on a specific silhouette. If they have made it to best – or worst – dressed lists, pay attention. The stylist that cost them a fortune has just done you a big favour and given you a shortcut to knowing what you should be looking for.

The paper-doll exercise is exposing but very worthwhile. Even if you are planning to go on an amazing diet and drop some weight before your next fashion splurge or big event, think about this: your basic silhouette doesn't really change that much. I have been 55 kilos and 65 kilos at different points in my life, and the styles that worked on me were the same – just in different sizes, and obviously I had more poodja woodja at 65 kilograms.

Your body shape is a given. Whether you are at your leanest or your biggest, the basic blueprint stays the same.

People who tend to carry weight on their thighs will always carry weight on their thighs. The same is true if you tend to stack it on around your tummy. If your shoulders are broad, that's a skeletal issue and it won't change.

This message is doubly important for brides-to-be. Sort this out at the beginning of the design process so that at least you know your dress is the right one for your silhouette, even if it does need to be fitted closer to the big day. (You know, if you get divorced later at least your dress will have been perfect. And that's quite satisfying when you're sitting around drinking way too much and tearing all those photos right down the middle.)

On your paper doll, draw a black line across the widest part of your body. The line might run from hip to hip, across your waist, across your shoulders, etc. This line is crucial because it is the strongest horizontal to mitigate when you choose an outfit.

Putting verticals to work

Now it's time to compare your silhouette to that of the standard industry sample body, Sheila. Pay attention to the vertical aspects here. Note how much of a height difference there is between you, 175-centimetre Liz and 164-centimetre Sheila. Is your torso longer than Sheila's, shorter, or the same? How about your legs? If you are blessed with long legs then you are indeed a lucky girl. As the vertical principle is fundamental to this process, height and length variances are very important.

Every time you add a horizontal line into an outfit, you are stripping 5 centimetres off your height. If you are too tall this can be helpful. However, if you are vertically challenged, this can be a big problem.

Draw vertical arrows where you need to add length to your body.

Remember that every time you tear a picture of a dress you love from a magazine, you are looking at it on 175-centimetre-tall Liz, who, let's face it, is not a standard human being. Aspiration versus reality. But we will try and trick the eye into seeing aspects of lofty Liz in you wherever we can.

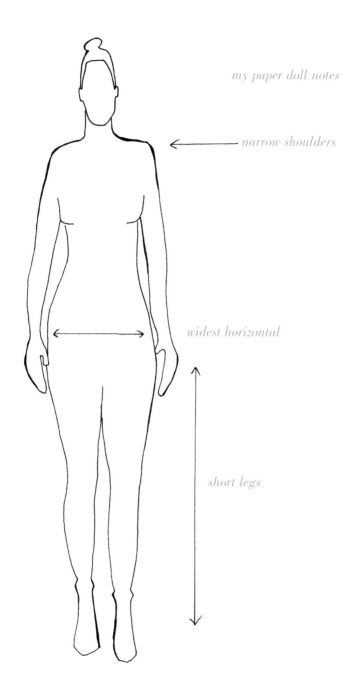

my paper doll notes

narrow shoulders

widest horizontal

short legs

VERTICALS AND HORIZONTALS

The deal breakers

The secret to an outfit working or not working all comes back to the vertical–horizontal principle. It's very straightforward:

* Verticals make you tall and thin.
* Horizontals make you short and stocky.
* Horizontals need to be eradicated as much as possible.

Working in television, where every single outfit is framed by a strong horizontal aspect, i.e. the screen shape, I have been fighting the battle against the horizontal for half my life. Every decision I make about clothing is based on how many verticals I can introduce in order to minimise the effect of the horizontal lines.

Similarly, when having your photo taken, try your best to get vertical-framed pictures rather than landscape shape because you are always going to look better in them. Brides, pay attention!

Keep in mind that:

* The broadest area of your body will be the strongest horizontal line.
* The shoulder area is a strong horizontal line.
* Any horizontals you can weed out of an outfit will help to strengthen the verticals and you will look taller and thinner.
* Vertical stripes and line details such as pleats and ruching can also become horizontals. En masse, they are more fence-like (horizontal) than ladder-like (vertical). For super-skinny Kate-shaped paper dolls, this can be used in a good way, to add perceived bulk. *Nobody is flattered by a fully ruched feature unless they are a size 8 or smaller.*

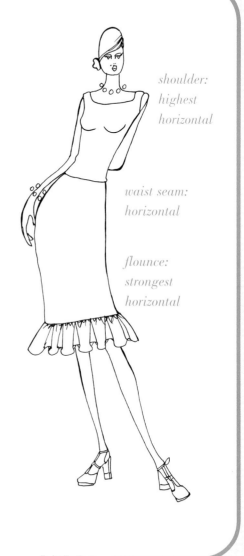

shoulder:
highest
horizontal

waist seam:
horizontal

flounce:
strongest
horizontal

If a design detail has to be horizontal, such as a trouser waistband for example, look at how loudly it is saying, 'Hello, look at me! I'm a horizontal.' Unless you have a tiny waist, why choose a contrast belt to make it shout even louder, when you could wear a belt the same colour or fabric? If you have broad shoulders, why choose a puff-sleeved shirt to increase the volume of the area, and its horizontal aspect? Why add the strong horizontal element of a detailed shoulder bag that sits at the hip line if that is your widest area?

Reduce your vision to 2D, like your paper doll, and look for verticals and horizontals.

Cut out the voice in your head that is being driven by marketing, and instead look at your clothing choices with only critical, scientific eyes. There are pieces in every collection that will satisfy both fashion dictates and logic, from Primark to Prada.

For every strong horizontal element you must find three verticals.

* Legs are our friends. They are strong verticals that can be recruited.
* Centre front detailing such as long jacket lapels, buttons on shirt fronts and trims can be used to add verticals.
* Darts, pleats and tucks, when used purposefully, can help.

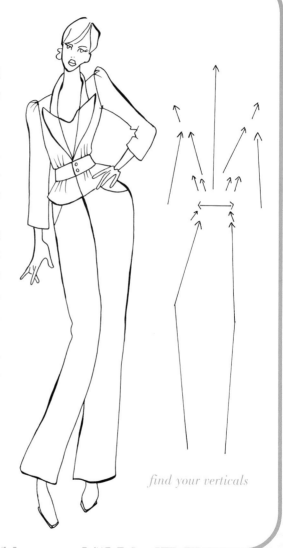

find your verticals

If you can mitigate a horizontal line, you should. Changing the harshness of the line introduces a vertical suggestion.

* Rather than going for a straight line, choose a curved line.
* V-shaped lines have more vertical emphasis than straight horizontals.
* Again, darts, pleats and tucks, used purposefully, can help.

*changing
lines*

Your Three Worst Enemies

Lurking within each of us is a dislike of something we find really physically unattractive about ourselves. For some it's thigh anxiety. For others it's a round tummy from the 5 kilos we would rather not be in constant companionship with, or a big bust, a small bust, no neck, sloping shoulders, short legs . . . I could go on all day. Sadly, for most of us it's a combination effect that does our heads in. We are going to seek these out now and name names.

Make mine the no-waist special, with the double helping of ex-breastfeeding bosoms, tuckshop arms and age anxiety, please. And I'm a normal height, size 10. Technically I am industry sample size. So I should be okay, but there are so many styles that just don't work on me.

There is some ancient Chinese wisdom that you need to use your enemy's energy to your own advantage. I'm sure that this is all well and good in the art of physical self-defence, so I would like to apply it to mental self-defence now. Stop letting your enemies defeat you, be they your legs or your bust, and harness their energies instead. *Acknowledge the features you want to disarm and work towards enhancing other aspects of your appearance.* Set this strategy as a certainty. It's time to acknowledge your issues and embrace them. (This is getting a bit LA now.)

Mere Mortal Tip #1
KNOW YOUR ENEMIES

Write down your three least appealing physical features, starting with the worst. If you are so overwhelmed by self-hatred that you can't make a short list, please ask your best friend, your sister or, if you're married, your mother-in-law, as she will always give a brutally honest appraisal of your flaws. If you have a daughter, she will be honest too – and you can make her do the housework as punishment if she gets too mean.

If you really, truly don't have three to list, bully for you.

Now take your paper-doll template and some colouring pens: a dark blue one, a medium blue one, and a light blue one. Using the dark blue pen, draw a band on your paper doll on the area of your Enemy #1. Use the medium blue pen to do the same for Enemy #2. And the light blue pen for Enemy #3.

The widest part of your body might not be Enemy #1: it is just the thing you least like about your body. For some people it might be a scar or fat ankles.

Your One Killer Feature

Remember Rapunzel? Yes, we know she was a princess who had great hair. That's it. For all we know, she had stretch marks, bad teeth and three legs. For that matter, she may have had a hideously hairy back. You get the picture.

The prince was so busy looking up that tower wall at her glossy gold locks that he didn't report back on anything else other than her One Killer Feature.

Jackie Kennedy apparently had bow legs and large hands. We remember her for stylish sunglasses highlighting a striking face.

Audrey Hepburn didn't like her large feet and flat chest. We remember this enduring style icon for her swanlike neck.

And have you ever noticed that Olivia Newton-John always wears boots or long trousers? Probably not. If you do a Google search you will see that she has great arms and shoulders, even now in her fifties, and many of her photos show them off.

Hopefully you already know what your One Killer Feature is, but some people get really baffled by this and look at *all their good assets* as equal. Jordan, are you paying attention? There is no equality in fashion.

Mere Mortal Tip #2
KNOW YOUR ONE
KILLER FEATURE

The wise choice is an outfit that highlights your One Killer Feature and also gives a gentle nod to your lesser better attributes. Obviously if you are blessed with a few natural wonders we wouldn't want to understate them too much.

Let's go back to your paper doll and use a yellow pen to highlight the most appealing area of your body: your One Killer Feature. This killer feature has to be the highlight of the journey towards your face when someone looks at you in your outfit. The closer to your face the One Killer Feature is, the easier the design process. The eye will have a better chance of staying at the top part of the body, and the verticals will be stronger for it. And in the coming chapters I'll show you how to make the eye do what you want it to.

THE THREE POINT PLAN

Can you wear it?

Even if all the design principles add up to a particular outfit being the best one for you, there's another important consideration: will you actually wear it?

The Three Point Plan revolves around your *personality*, the *environment* and the *design*, which all need to be in balance or you will definitely do one of two things: a) never wear the outfit, or b) wear it and be extremely uncomfortable in it.

It is pointless to dress up as a princess if you are going to behave like the hired help all night. It is pointless to have a gown made if you are a trousers-wearing kind of person. It's pointless to buy into trends and wear styles that *theoretically* work if you just don't like them.

For me, it's shirts. I don't feel like me in them and although from time to time I get swayed into thinking that maybe I am a shirt-wearing kind of girl, it always turns out that I am not. There is every good reason for me to see the value in the design of a shirt that works on my frame, but I just don't like wearing shirts. I do like them on other people, though.

I have a friend who simply will not consider polonecks. Ever.

Alannah Hill doesn't wear trousers. Only dresses and skirts.

And that is so fine.

Apply all three aspects of the Three Point Plan to choosing your purchases.

1 Is it in character for you?
2 Is it appropriate for the occasion?
3 Does the design work for your body?

Rather than forcing you to wear the Emperor's New Clothes, this book is about empowering you to have confidence and feel good about your own wardrobe choices.

Star Shape

The new, improved you

So now that you know your basic silhouette, One Killer Feature and Three Worst Enemies, you can start to work through the options that are going to make you look like a better version of you.

It's a bit like going to the fridge and knowing you are allergic to some things in there, intolerant to others and fine about a few key ingredients that are good for you.

Mere Mortal Tip #3
PEOPLE HAVE LAZY EYES

Here is the dish on how it all goes together.

The more you draw attention to your One Killer Feature and make it easier for the eye to travel up the silhouette to your face, ignoring all your horizontal issues, the better you will look. This is because people have lazy eyes.

A full-length outfit will always make you look taller and thinner than a shorter one because there is one less horizontal to work with.

The lazy eye will always find its way most easily to an obvious highlight or strong feature, pale colour or shiny surface.

*draw attention to your
One Killer Feature*

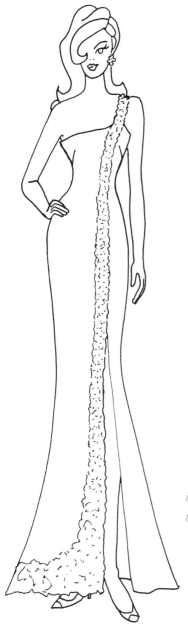

If you can force the eye up towards your face, you will immediately appear taller and leaner. The best way to do this is to ensure an uninterrupted flow from hem to hairdo.

Mere Mortal Tip #4

ALWAYS AIM TO KEEP THE EYE TRAVELLING UPWARDS

use decoration to keep the eye travelling up

One very effective way to keep the eye travelling up towards your face is to use similar points of interest in your outfit: the eye will try to match them, and will travel upwards to do this.

Think sparkly crystal-encrusted shoes, leading to a divine sparkly hand-bag at hip level, leading to knock-out diamond chandelier earrings. That's Dot to Dot at work. In eveningwear it is easier to use this strategy because a sparkle can be recruited for maximum effect. In daywear you might use the same principle with colour.

Mere Mortal Tip #5
APPLY THE DOT TO DOT PRINCIPLE

use similar points of interest

LIGHT AND DARK

The shapers

The use of block colour, highlight colours, pale colours and light-reflecting fabrics creates optical illusions to be taken into consideration. The same design made in different colours can read totally differently on the same body. The cardinal points are:

* Dark areas are minimised.
* Light areas are maximised or enhanced to the power of one size extra.

This is why we all love the Little Black Dress.

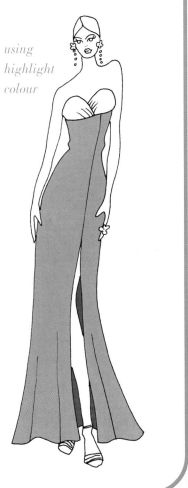

using highlight colour

The same designs made in different colours can read totally differently on the same body, but wearing a very pale colour makes you look one size larger. If you are very waif-like, use this strategy to add bulk to your frame.

A light-coloured shirt with a dark skirt will always be a more slimming look than the reverse. This is because the eye is kept high with a pale colour up top, reinforcing the vertical. So don't feel you need to wear only dark colours in tops if you are heavier in that area.

Patterned fabrics act much like pale shades in that they have the same overall effect, maximising the area where they are placed. They can even serve to make the area look broader if there are many horizontal aspects in the pattern or the fabric has a busy weave such as a hound's-tooth check.

Plaids throw up all manner of horizontals and verticals and their use should be thought through very carefully. It's always most flattering to use checks as highlight areas only rather than as an overall garment, unless Kate is your paper doll.

plaid and plain

pattern placement

The use of macro prints — those with large design elements — is another tricky decision. Placed well, a pattern can give an optical illusion that is flattering, but placed badly it can make your enemies even worse. As most off-the-rack garments are not cut with fabric pattern placement as a priority, the placement is random, so flip through the garments and really look at what the pattern is doing to the design lines before you try it on. The same design might look very different on you in the very next garment on the rack.

Putting your One Killer Feature to work

The key to dressing like a star is to know exactly what to do with your One Killer Feature, how to enhance it with other good attributes, and how to downplay your less-loved aspects. Let's look at the body-specific principles that cover daywear. This is where you can enlist the paper dolls to play with. Try the shapes out on them so you can see clearly whether they work. In chapters 4 and 5 you can refine the process of applying the principles to the areas of racing wear and eveningwear, and in chapter 6 for brides. For now, let's review the basics.

Killer Feature: legs galore

In daywear, the best way to play up killer legs is to wear a skirt with a hem that rests just under the knee where the calf is at its narrowest. The eye has the opportunity to work up from a great shoe, through a great calf and then it travels north, up the body.

determining skirt length

A general rule of thumb is that the wider the area at the hemline, the shorter the legs will appear. You want an overall vertical effect, not a horizontal.

Pleats are worth mentioning. Although the pressed folds are technically running in a vertical direction, their overall accumulation to the eye can look horizontal if there are a lot of them. When you see striped detail on any garment ask yourself whether it has a *fence* or *ladder* effect. For example, fully pleated skirts say *fence* (a horizontal effect), whereas a couple of feature pleats can say *ladder* (a vertical effect that leads the eye upward).

In eveningwear, a strong vertical split, Liz Hurley-style, can be used to throw a clear vertical message into a gown.

Narrow-legged trousers are best for you. They highlight the fact that you can wear them and that you're not hiding anything alarming in them. Detailing at the hip area, such as little pocket flaps, tabs or stitching can only work on Legs Galore as the long journey up through the body finds a meaningful resting spot before heading north to the face.

When it comes to jackets and shirts, longer ones work best on Legs Galore. For you there is enough of a distance from hem to hip to balance these kinds of garments.

Super-skinny trousers only really work on super-skinny women, and even then they don't look particularly flattering. If you're going for a classic star look, fitted and lean is always better and way classier than painted-on trousers. It's a fine line that creates the difference between looking like you are channelling Cameron Diaz or channelling Posh on a thin day.

Shoes are important here because you can further elongate the legs by making sure any detail on the shoe is at the toe end. Avoid ankle straps. They cut the foot down and break the eye's journey between toe and knee.

The principle is this: the closer to your face the party is, the taller you will seem. We don't want the eye to drop downwards if it can be avoided. Obviously, if you are really, really tall and want to play down your height, reverse this rule to your advantage.

Killer Feature: great hips and thighs

Tulip skirts are great on slim hips. That extra bulk in the design at the rear adds volume you can support.

Little design details or pocket flaps are good for the same reason. You are trying to highlight that you are small in the area and embellishment is one way to do this. Feature belts are also effective.

palazzo and manstyle trousers

Trousers are best in a slouchy manstyle or simple palazzo shape in the manner of Katharine Hepburn, to highlight your small bottom.

Avoid higher waistlines. They introduce a squareness to the torso, which will actually make you look like a boy. I'm not saying you have to go super low-slung, either, but a waist somewhere between the belly button and the high hip bone will work best.

Having smaller hips allows you a little grace for offsetting the top of your body, so you will be more able to use shiny fabrics, colour, pale shades or prints through the skirt area than other women.

Killer Feature: smaller waist

Well, aren't you the lucky one?

If you have a small waist, the question is: smaller compared to your bust or your hips or both?

Refer to your paper doll again to determine whether your bust or hips are wider than your waist. For instance, your *actual* bust measurement may be larger than your hips, but it could be projected forward so the hip *appears* wider overall. And that's what counts: the widest point on your paper-doll silhouette.

If your bust is bigger than your hips and your waist is the smallest horizontal in the body you can afford to *carefully* take attention to the hip and waist to downplay the bust. Whether this is with well-placed draping, colour, fabric contrast or embellishment is up to you. There are designs in chapter 9, Star Scape (the Look Book), that illustrate this.

emphasising the waist

You could consider breaking the garment at waist level, maybe with a feature belt or a trim. The point is that the waist should be a focus area in the outfit before the eye travels to the face.

Trousers are best with a true or slightly lower than true waist (which is about 1 centimetre higher than the belly button). Not high, because that swings the attention towards your busty horizontals. Choose leg shapes that flare ever so slightly from the hip so that the silhouette in 2D is basically like a long, slim A-line skirt. This shape will balance the fuller bust.

The same is true of skirt shapes: slimmer A-line and straight skirts will be your best choices. The hem should sit just below the knee, at the slimmest part of the calf. This gives the suggestion of longer legs. If you are after a shorter skirt, the point slightly above the knee where the thigh is still lean is the best choice.

If your hips are bigger than your bust and your waist is the smallest horizontal in the body, you are lucky because the attention can be at waist point and above. Nice and close to the face.

choose your skirt length wisely

Skirts that fall easily over the hips, such as A-lines, are good. In a full-length gown you could look at a princess line or even the full-blown meringue. You can hide larger hips under a meringue, so there is a place in the world for these frocks. Think of the Dior New Look that took over fashion at the end of World War II, with a very full skirt and a very small waist. It doesn't work at all unless the small waist controls the dynamic. You might just be Grace Kelly after all.

You should always err towards longer skirts as short skirts will only give weight to the hip horizontal.

For people who have the small waist/bigger hip scenario, trousers are often hard to find. Look for front details such as cutaway slanted pockets, or almost-vertical welt pockets to move the eye upwards. Avoid back pockets, and if you are buying jeans look for pockets that sit closer to the waist rather than lower across the fullest part of your bottom.

full skirt for fuller hips

long torso emphasised

long torso concealed

Trousers and skirts in a deeper hue than the top half of the outfit are always good as they keep the attention moving upwards.

If you have a long torso with a small waist, dresses are going to work best on you. The point is to conceal where the torso ends and the legs start. So listen up, long-torso people: *trousers are not your friend*. I understand that you want to wear them, but they just will never look flattering. Period.

Choose under-bust detail that relies on your small waist to carry the look. Avoid lower-hip detail if you have a long torso as it underscores it.

*a lower than
true-waist seam*

People who have a long torso with a smaller waist compared to hip can wear waistbands that are cut ever so slightly higher. This gives more perceived leg length and less length in the torso.

Skirt lengths need to play on the optical illusion principle. It's always better to conceal the knee so that the question of just where your legs actually start is removed.

If you have a short torso with a small waist, lower-waisted trousers are going to be better on you as that will open up the torso area, making it appear longer.

Mere Mortal Tip #7
THE LAZY EYE GETS
DISTRACTED EASILY

Choose belt details that hit ever so slightly below the true waist, so that the upper torso length is increased a little.

When choosing a dress, look for a lower waistline that steals a little length from the skirt to the body. Robbing Peter to pay Paul. Another option is to not 'break' at the waist, but continue the skirt line right up under the bust, keeping the whole area clean and simple.

Shorter skirts will be good for you if you have the legs to carry the look, as the shortness of the torso can be balanced with a long, leggy vertical in the bottom half.

It's important to remember that the lazy eye will be distracted easily. Do you look at Marmite sandwiches when there is devil's food cake on the table? Probably not. It's the same principle at work here.

It's all about using your embellishment such as trims, texture and contrast to the best advantage. Place it where it forces the lazy eye to linger or move vertically. Keep it to one area of your outfit if you can, but use the Dot to Dot principle if you can't.

Killer Feature: great back

It is very important that if you choose to highlight your back and make it the hero of an outfit, you know this: *you can have a low back or you can have a low front but you can't have both.*

Somehow this thing needs to stay on and having it both ways will be problematic no matter how many packets of Tapeits you buy. Choosing a low-cut back will also mean you are restricted by what underwear you can wear. If you can get away without needing a bra, that's great. If you need to wear a bra, try Liftits first (see the Wardrobe Mistress's Kit on p. 188) before ruling the backless scenario out because they offer a good amount of support. If Liftits are not for you, then you should start looking for a bra that sits quite low at the back and work the design around it. Fine Lines have a great Strapless Backless Bustier that is good if you are fairly small-waisted as it features a low-dipping back but lots of support as well.

Given that low back features are more for night-time than daytime, if your back is your One Killer Feature you should rely on your second choice for daywear.

Killer Feature: great bust

Assuming we are working on the same page here and you don't consider having Pamela Anderson breasts a killer feature, we can do this. That's not so much killer in the good sense as killer in the gentlemen's club sense. With me?

emphasising the bust with tucks

If your bust is your One Killer Feature, the lazy eye is working with you because the higher the killer feature is on the body, the further the eye travels from the floor, adding precious centimetres to your frame. Hooray.

The best place for a great bust highlight is the line directly under it, where the band on the bottom of your bra sits. This horizontal can be curved slightly upwards from the waist, meeting at the centre of the bust if that design line works for you: it's better for those with wider hips. Or the line can be straight across like your bra, which is better for those with smaller hips.

Mere Mortal Tip #8
THE LAZY EYE SEES THINGS
IN A SIMPLISTIC WAY:
WIDE AREA OF BODY;
LESS WIDE AREA OF BODY

I have found that with most women, this space around the high rib cage is usually quite slim in comparison to the waist and bust, which are more likely to wear the fat stores. So it's a great place for embellishment to highlight the bust. Also, little tucks or gathers under the bust can look really good.

The use of colour breaks or contrast fabrics or trims can highlight the bust without making the grand 'Hello, look at my breasts!' statement.

If you are thinking about shirting, make sure that the buttons are positioned to show some cleavage without looking trashy. Three centimetres either way can be the difference between grandma and bimbo, so really look at the button position and if it is wrong, walk away. It can't be fixed and if you think that you might just pop a safety pin in there for modesty, please don't. It never looks right. The correct position for the top button to have buttoned up is two centimetres above the centre band of your bra, which should be a fairly narrow band in order to maximise your décolletage.

Blouses that have horizontal gathers from the centre front band can work well as a bust highlight, too. They are usually in fashion for about ten minutes, though, so if it's longevity you are thinking about, it is probably better to stay classic.

Empire line dresses, baby dolls and other girly shapes that feature the bust and gloss over the waist are great. With these shapes, it's all about the bust and everything else becomes irrelevant. Perfect.

Your best necklines are versions of the square shape as the strong horizontal moves the eye across the chest area, but the verticals also encourage it up towards the face.

*position your
shoulder straps for
maximum effect*

If we count on the lazy eye to see the simple lines of wide and less wide areas of the torso, we should be aware of manipulating the design so that one part of our body takes the fall to make another part look better.

Simple changes, such as altering the distance that shoulder straps are set apart, can make the waist seem narrower or wider. They can also make the shoulders seem broader or narrower.

Killer Feature: great shoulders and neck

Having great shoulders is a blessing because this feature is so close to the face.

Princess Mary of Denmark's wedding gown featured a simple boat neck, which was clean and broad. It is a great choice for anyone who has the benefit of angular shoulders and it balances a long neck.

A similar outcome is achieved with the high squared-off boat neck, or the very wide boat neck popular in the early 1960s that sat just off the shoulders, creating a great horizontal at the shoulder. Very Audrey Hepburn in *Roman Holiday*.

Strapless dresses and fine spaghetti straps will work on you and you will not look like Princess Fiona, I promise. Look at adding embellishment around the straps and necklines of your dresses if you are trying to conceal bigger hips. Or if you are trying to play down a full bust, avoid the embellishment and stick with a flattering neckline alone.

boat neckline

square neckline

rounded-off square neckline

deep square neckline

Necklines for all of us

If your bust is large keep your neckline as simple as you can and keep the fabrication matte. Remember to always make the focus of the outfit your One Killer Feature.

When working out how low-cut is appropriate, look in the mirror and be very critical about your neck.

If your neck is short, take your neckline lower to give the eye more vertical movement through the thorax. Twice the neck length is a good rule of thumb. Look at the photograph you made your paper doll from and you will be able to clearly judge the length of your neck in relation to the rest of your body.

If your neck is long, you can afford to have a higher neckline as the verticals are already going your way.

If you have a short torso and wish to wear a rounded-off square neckline, be very careful about the depth as having it too low will shorten your body further. It's about balance. Drawing different depths of neckline on your paper doll will be helpful, as you can see – without going through the pain of trying on a single garment – what is going to work.

Sloping shoulders can be helped by a broad, deep V neckline, which can play up décolletage while putting a handy vertical aspect into the equation.

And remember, for both the rounded-off square neckline and the deep V, the wider the strap separation, the smaller the waist will be perceived to be. On wide-set straps I like to use bra-strap keepers so that everything stays together; the tautness of the bra straps offers a little more safety for slippery dress straps.

A flattering, simple neckline for all of us is my personal favourite, the low rounded-off square neckline. It can work well, particularly if you have sloping shoulders, as it will help correct them with a strong horizontal. It embraces the whole low-cut aspect of a strapless garment, but has straps that take the eye upward to the face. With a little cap sleeve covering the often problematic bicep area, it becomes a most flattering shape and one that Roland Mouret recruited for his famous Galaxy Dress. The implied triangle pointing to the diminished waist makes women seem more like 1950s sirens and less like their normal selves.

the Galaxy dress

Sleeves for all of us

Sleeves in daywear can be great for slimming the arms and hiding tuckshop issues, and are mandatory for many of us who are in sensible jobs.

The ultimate sleeve will always be the three-quarter-length fitted sleeve as it doesn't add bulk. Little details such as trims or buttons can be helpful if you are trying to add horizontals at the hip area to highlight a small waist or take attention away from a problematic bust. Otherwise, keep it simple.

Puff sleeves, while very sweet, are going to strip credibility from those of us who need to look particularly chic. They have an aspect of Little Red Riding Hood about them. But they do have the benefit of adding volume above the waist area, thereby reducing the perceived waist size. I strongly recommend that if you are over forty, forget puff sleeves altogether. It's a harsh world.

bell sleeve   *tulip sleeve*   *leg o'mutton sleeve*

You could, however, employ a little gathering or pleating strictly at the sleeve head, which is more Scarlett O'Hara and less Little Red Riding Hood. This detail, being close to the face, will also be useful in keeping the attention at the top of the body, which is always a good idea.

The bell sleeve, tulip sleeve, and the big daddy of them all, the leg o' mutton sleeve, should be worn only after giving the matter great consideration. There is so much volume being added into the picture that you must be very clear that your torso can carry it. The last thing you want to be is a block of fabric with a body in it. Where is the killer feature here? Is it lost in the overwhelming aspect of sleeve? There is a very sound reason that these shapes come in and out of fashion.

Consider where the bulkiest part of the sleeve is, and if it falls where you are also bulky, forget it.

* **Tulip sleeves and long bell sleeves** can be worn by people with slim hips.
* **Bell sleeves** will not work if you have a larger waist.
* **Puff sleeves** cannot be worn by people with broad shoulders.
* **Short puff sleeves** which gather into a band are bad for big busts.
* **Three-quarter-length fitted sleeves** are good for practically everybody.

Killer Features:
a summary of the basics

This is where it all comes together. You should now have a good idea of the basic lines and shapes that will work on your One Killer Feature. The differences of torso length and leg length, as well as the variations in the runner-up killer features, will come into play as you read on through this breakdown. When I say 'with consideration, settle for' I am referring directly to these attributes as they will affect the outcome of how the style looks on you.

Killer Feature: legs galore

Aim for: shorter skirts, straight skirts, slim trousers, textural difference in the lower half, slash pockets at the hip.

With consideration, settle for: A-line skirts that finish at a narrow point of the calf, cuff detail on sleeves, subtle belts.

Avoid: pleated skirts, collar detail, bright or patterned top halves.

Killer Feature: great hips and thighs

Aim for: feature cuffs on sleeves, bell sleeves, tulip skirts, slightly lower waistlines, slim trousers and skirts, detail at the high hip area, stronger patterns or colour in the bottom half, shorter skirts, feature belts that sit on the high hip bone, shapeless tops that finish at the hip, jackets that finish at the hip, swing jackets that finish at the high hip.

With consideration, settle for: monochromatic outfits, subtle belts, pleats.

Avoid: high waistlines, strong detail or prints above the waist, super-fitted above the hip, boleros and short jackets.

Killer Feature: smaller waist

Aim for: feature belts, A-line or full skirts, slimline or slightly flared trousers, boleros, jackets that finish at high hip bone, elbow-length sleeves, tulip sleeves, strapless dresses or those that leave the shoulders clear.

With consideration, settle for: straight skirts, subtle belts.

Avoid: baby dolls and shapeless dresses, strong detail at the neck area, super skinny trousers.

Killer Feature: great back

Aim for: using this killer feature for evening and holiday dressing or you will look trashy; for daywear, try draping at the back, detailed back straps, high neckline at the front.

With consideration, settle for: halter styles or spaghetti straps.

Avoid: low fronts with your low backs, bright or pale lower halves.

Killer Feature: great bust

Aim for: squared-off round necklines, halter and bikini shapes for appropriate occasions, puff sleeves, cap sleeves, bust detail with trims, darting, gathering or contrast fabrics, baby doll and empire-line dresses, darker lower halves, boleros and shorter jackets.

With consideration, settle for: strong collar detail, round necks.

Avoid: shirts that button in the wrong position, feature belts, high necklines, block knits that offer no variation at the bust area.

Killer Feature: great shoulders and neck

Aim for: wide boat necks, deep V necklines, embellishment at the neck area, strapless dresses or those that expose the skin of the shoulder area, interesting collar detail, puff sleeves, cap sleeves, darker bottom halves, shawl-collared jackets.

With consideration, settle for: round necklines, subtle belts.

Avoid: closed necklines, scarves, detailing anywhere lower than the bust area of the outfit, feature belts, bright or busy lower halves.

Worst Enemies: a summary of the basics

Again, the two runner-up worst enemies will affect how well certain styles work on you. The idea is to consider the design concepts from the Killer Features list, playing up your good points, while paying attention to the shape warnings in the Worst Enemies list. The marriage of the two scenarios will give you the best styles for your silhouette.

Worst Enemy: short legs, longer torso

Aim for: shapeless tunic tops to disguise where the legs actually start, straight skirts, skirts and dresses in preference to trousers, shoes that match your trousers or nude shoes for skirts, shorter jackets, and swing jackets with dresses.

With consideration, settle for: single pleats in a skirt, A-line or full skirts.

Avoid: cuffs on trousers, wide-legged trousers, hipster anything, three-quarter-length trousers, skirts above the knee, long jackets, ankle straps on shoes.

Worst Enemy: short torso

Aim for: lower-waisted clothes and hipsters, lower belt detail, hip pocket detail, paler or patterned top halves, capri trousers, collar detail.

With consideration, settle for: shorts, skirts that fall from a fitted basque, a few well-placed pleats, fitted shirts left untucked.

Avoid: high-waisted anything, wide belts, feature belts.

Worst Enemy: chunky arms

Aim for: three-quarter-length sleeves with minimum detail, darker tones.

With consideration, settle for: cuff detail, wraps and boleros.

Avoid: puff sleeves, bare arms, strong bust detail, patterned fabric for sleeves.

Worst Enemy: no waist

Aim for: baby doll shapes, shifts, empire-line dresses and tunics, swing jackets, detail at the collar area, short or cap sleeves, slightly flared trousers, A-line skirts, jackets that finish at the true hip.

With consideration, settle for: shorts, fitted shirts left untucked, darker top half than lower half.

Avoid: two-piece outfits, high-waisted anything, slimline trousers, straight skirts, short tops, short jackets and boleros, belts of any kind, sleeves that finish at the waist.

Worst Enemy: large hips

Aim for: darker, matte lower halves, A-line skirts, straight-leg trousers with waistlines slightly lower than true, bust detail, collar area detail, fitted princess-line dresses that sweep past the hips, longer skirts.

With consideration, settle for: puff sleeves, very full skirts.

Avoid: clingy or shiny fabrics, detail of any kind at the hip area, fitted straight skirts or dresses, wide-legged trousers, belts, short tops or anything that stops at the high hip.

Worst Enemy: large bust

Aim for: matte, darker area at the bust, longer sleeves, boat neck or higher wide V-shaped necklines.

With consideration, settle for: well-placed dart treatment at the bust, paler or patterned bottom halves, contrast collar and cuffs.

Avoid: detail or shiny fabric at the bust, puff sleeves, feature belts, double-breasted jackets, boleros.

Worst Enemy: broad shoulders

Aim for: raglan sleeves (see page 75), deeper angled V-necks, longer jackets that button at the waist, longer tulip sleeves or bell sleeves.

With consideration, settle for: tiny cap sleeves for eveningwear, lower bust detail, mid-torso detail, paler or patterned lower halves, feature buttons.

Avoid: halter-necks, puff sleeves, short sleeves.

Worst Enemy: short neck

Aim for: lower necklines, deeper angled V-necks, long scarves, jackets that button at the waist, halter-necks.

With consideration, settle for: bust detail, feature belts.

Avoid: high necklines, puff sleeves, collar detail, turtlenecks.

Star style: which star are you?

At this point you will have a better idea of the types of garments that your body will look best in.

If you are the shapeless shift type, with no waist, you might be a 1920s Louise Brooks, a 1960s Edie Sedgwick or a millennium Sienna Miller.

If you are a curvaceous type you might like to take a leaf out of 1950s Veronica Lake's book, or that of Elizabeth Taylor or Catherine Zeta-Jones.

For some of you it's going to be Oprah, and for others Helen Mirren.

And for a lucky few it really will be Mischa Barton, and you can afford to dress just like her.

The point is that if you can identify a star who has emphasised the same One Killer Feature, or worn a particular style of clothing that has now come to your attention, there is a good chance that she has a similar basic body shape. Then you can take a shortcut to see what iconic styles are working on her body. Whether for red carpet or for daytime, these looks are there to be plundered and adapted for your life and your big events.

This continues on to makeup and hair choices too, as you will probably find that modern styles will need a slight adaptation to make the outfits translate. I'm not talking full-blown costume drama, of course. It could be as simple as a heavy top eyeliner and ruby lipstick that says Liz Taylor in *Cat on a Hot Tin Roof*, or smoky eyes and nude lips that says Twiggy. Simple touches like that can give the look a polish.

Star bright: the colour issue

A great tool for updating an established star look is by the use of colour. Maggie in *Cat on a Hot Tin Roof* may be roughly where your style is heading, but perhaps black is not your colour. A simple change of hue can change the personality of the outfit. Temptress in black to sweetness in raspberry. The shape remains, the verticals and horizontals are the same, but the voice of the outfit has changed.

People have made big business out of colour theory and the art of matching people with their palettes. I don't believe in the value of declaring someone is 'spring' and someone else is 'autumn'. If you are spring and all the fashion colours in store are mustards, olives and terracottas, are you supposed to go nude for the season?

I have always found that people like what they like. They are comfortable and happy in some colours and most uncomfortable in others. Listen acutely, though, when you get a compliment. When someone tells you that you look radiant or particularly beautiful in something, pay attention to what colour you are wearing that day. It's probably your best hue.

If you love to wear black, but your favourite and most complimented colour is green, for example, then perhaps accessorise with that colour. Or have an aspect or print in the outfit in green. You don't have to commit to the glorious technicolor rainbow; many people feel overstated in head-to-toe colour. But punctuations of colour can inject freshness into a dark ensemble and also give you a fine reason to have to buy a great handbag or shoes. Hues of the various colours in the wheel can be the best choice for many of us, as they inject a visual personality without shouting it to the world.

The one place to wear colour if you are confident enough, and have the reason to be there, is the red carpet. Photographers *always* gravitate towards it because it will read well in a photo. The true way to tell when a star has made it is when she can afford to wear black to the Oscars and still be photographed.

The most flattering colour for fair skin tones is blue. Because this skin colour has flushes of pinks and yellows, most people have an aspect of blue as the opposite area in the colour wheel. Therefore, blue makes you look healthier, brighter and absolutely lovely in a photograph.

Red gives a charge of energy to an outfit and makes a strong statement, so wear it if you know that's what you need.

The citrus palette of yellow, orange and lime is very hard for many people to wear. These are much better as punctuations and are best kept away from the face, as the reflected light can be quite sickly.

And while we are on *sickly*, I caution you from embracing the fashion forces that push us towards the neutral zone of taupe, grey, putty, donkey (a grey-brown), and anything else that lacks pigment. If these hues are close to your face they will drain the colour from you. So make sure you either wear strong enough makeup to accommodate that, or break the bleakness with a colour accent. A necklace, scarf or stronger-coloured shoulder bag worn high can offset the colour drain.

The thing about colour is this: you could probably wear any colour or hue you like and feel confident, but you should really think about how much hue is enough hue, and how much is overpowering with regards to the Three Point Plan on page 26. It's about knowing you *will* wear the outfit because you have balanced the occasion, your character and the design choice.

The last word on colour is this: don't match your makeup to your clothing. *Ever.* Wear makeup tones that *complement* your clothing, but don't do the matchy-matchy thing because you will make yourself look ten years older at least. This look is 1980s in a bad way; not in a cool way. If in doubt, go neutral. Go smokier, go lighter, but never go matchy.

Star Light

Separates anxiety

I love a frock. I do. There are so many design reasons to choose to wear a dress over any other type of garment.

But, having said that, I know that there are days when you just want to wear trousers, occasions when a suit is imperative, and how many of us can live happily ever after without our favourite jeans? Separates are very much a part of the landscape for daywear, because of their supposed versatility. The big issue is to make sure you buy pieces that are *actually* versatile. The danger is that by purchasing garments separately, you can't see how the balance and colour will work in the overall outfit. Until you get home, that is. And often that's when you realise that the piece you have just exceeded your credit limit for actually doesn't really work with anything.

I have a green cardigan that I bought in 2001. It is the most beautiful green and theoretically should look wonderful over lots of my clothes. But it doesn't. It is not quite the right green. So I keep it there in case one day the right dress turns up to take it out of the wardrobe. I believe we all have these lovely but useless garments that take up valuable space and make us feel guilty.

Cut your losses now and plan your day wardrobe.

Keep your One Killer Feature at the front of your mind. The pieces you have to actively seek out are those that will highlight your assets. The other pieces are almost fillers.

You should aim to have only one highlight area in an outfit. Whether this is a signature piece or a detailed area, limit it to one. If you flip through celebrity pictures you will notice that the successful looks are those that have limited use of killer accessories or signature pieces.

Trousers

The principles at work with long trousers are basically the same as those of the longer skirt in an evening-gown scenario. The eye needs to travel up the body to the killer feature. Whether we use flares as we do mermaid skirts, palazzo pants as we do A-line skirts, or straight-legged trousers as we do a straight skirt is a matter of design choice. The same overall silhouette principles apply.

Shorts take the design place of mini skirts, and culottes – ah, yes, culottes – take the place of shorter A-line skirts. It's very simple and yet so many women get it wrong.

Let's be realistic. The most fashion-forward shape of trousers is determined by designers. Therefore the shape of the season will only work on *some* women. The rest of us have to accept our limitations and make an enlightened choice about what shape of trouser will work on us.
Or wear a skirt.

Keep the waist clear of detail, particularly if you intend to wear your blouse or knit over trousers. Less bumps and lumps are better because that keeps the eye away from the tummy area, which for a good

Mere Mortal Tip #9

THE SIMPLER THE WAIST AREA, THE MORE FLATTERING THE DESIGN

many of us is not a killer feature. Pockets and detail around the hip and waist area need to be given great consideration, as it is likely that unless the pockets are running vertically they will add bulk and busy-ness.

Cuffs shorten the leg. End of story.

Pressed creases down the front of the legs add verticals if you feel that this look, which goes in and out of fashion every half an hour, is one that you like.

I have never yet dressed a woman who benefited from pleats in the front of her trousers.

Consider low-, mid- or high-waisted design lines as you would in a skirt. High-waisted may be the flavour of the minute, but do you look too short through the torso if you wear them? Can you balance a high waistline with the rest of the outfit? Does a high waist make your bottom look bigger? A broader bottom will always be better in slightly flared trousers with tops that float over the fullest part.

Stay with matte fabrics wherever possible, as sheen around the curves of an average bottom is never going to be a good look.

Medium-weight fabrics offer some support and can hide lumpy cellulite. Heavier weight fabrics, such as tweeds, no matter how fashionable, are only going to add bulk, which most of us do not want. Remember the principle of keeping the eye travelling upwards when choosing weaves and textures for trousers. The simpler the better, unless you are rake thin.

If you are wafer thin, and you don't like it, avoid super-fitted shapes which will emphasise your thinness. It is better for you to head towards a palazzo shape, which fools the eye into thinking you are beefier than you really are. Go for textures and weaves that are a little busy to broaden the area. Paler hues will also help.

As a general rule, keep the detail to one area of the body, preferably the higher end, of course. This will be determined by your One Killer Feature.

The back pockets on jeans are something that have fascinated me for years. Their shape and placement is crucial. Have a look with honest eyes. Too far apart and they make the hips look wider. Too low and they make the bottom look long. Too high and they make the derriere look hideously large. It's a total danger area, and the question 'Does my bum look big in these?' must be asked when trying on denim. Sadly, it's very hard to judge for yourself as you can't twist around properly.

Take a digital camera, or your mobile-phone camera, and your best shopping buddy as photographer when you are buying jeans. The back pockets should never be positioned at the fullest part of your bottom.

As a rule, the straighter the leg, the darker the denim and the less detailed the pockets, the more flattering the look.

And while we are on darkness, black opaque tights read as super skinny trousers. So treat them that way when you wear them with tunics and mini dresses. They deliver strong verticals to the outfit and should be regarded as helpful design tools.

With non-denim trousers, the cleaner the silhouette the better the look. If you flip through any magazine you are going to see celebrities in trousers that are fitted, quiet and uncluttered with detail. You are going to see high heels to add length to the legs or ballet pumps with a little fine ankle showing.

Trouser length should be almost to the ground but never touching it. Determine the length in the highest heels you are likely to wear, and aim for 2 centimetres off the ground. Your toes should be visible, but not the flesh of the heels.

What I am urging you to do is really think it through. Aim for the simplest trousers you can find, according to the silhouette that works for your hips and thighs. If you are uncertain that a pair is the right choice then don't go there. It is so much easier to get a skirt or a dress right.

Skirts

With a skirt there is no camel toe. No tight fork. No VPL or muffinery. And lots of deception available for keeping the elusive leg length a mystery, because the actual crotch level is concealed. Skirts win the flattering race hands down. It's no surprise that kilts look so good on men – the true details of their inadequacies are hidden.

There are two main considerations about skirts.

The first is the length, which should be determined by making sure that the distance from waist to hem is at least twice the distance from waist to shoulder. This is the 1:2 balance, a design tool employed by designers since the 1920s, and it works. It gives the eye the best opportunity to create flattering verticals for you. Ideally, you should position the hem at the point just above or just below the broadest part of the calf.

The second is the width. The wider the line at the hem, the smaller the waist will be perceived to be. But before you rush out and buy great swishy skirts, also remember that we are aiming to create outfits with interest at the top part of the body, so *think your bodice options through first*, and then choose the skirt that will work with them.

Skirts that feature front-buttoning detail or a couple of well-placed pleats will add length to shorter bodies and also mitigate a long torso.

Tiered skirts, while useful to hide broader hips, can be problematic when too many horizontals are added. So if you are looking at these, consider the 5 centimetres off your height per horizontal line rule. Darker plains rather than busy prints will be a better option, unless you are very tall and want to appear shorter.

Tulip skirts are ideal for people who have slim hips, as they can afford the extra volume at that area. If you are blessed with a small waist as well, belt it for even more definition.

Jackets

The design lines of a jacket can add verticals or dramatically change your shape to a block in one fell swoop.

The same principles of verticals and horizontals apply to the neckline, bodice shape and sleeve choices, but there are some other factors at work here as well.

The fitted jacket was a design developed for men. Who don't have breasts. As a concept it's already flawed, and the odds of creating a successful look are therefore stacked up against us.

The width across the shoulders should serve to make the waist look smaller. A small shoulder pad can do wonders for a waist, particularly if you have narrow or sloping shoulders. No Joan Collins behaviour here, though, please. Also try low funnel-neck lapels, like Jackie Kennedy's in her best White House years. Wide, curving lapels and zip-through shapes can help a narrow-shouldered person, and if you are lacking a waist as well you can even consider the bomber style, with epaulettes too if you like them.

A softer shoulder line allows the vertical of the lapels to take the spotlight, so this is a better choice if you have broader shoulders. Raglan sleeves and kimono shapes will also help to minimise strong shoulders. Detailing, such as binding on lapels or contrast lapels, equestrian style, can also help to reinforce the verticals for broad-shouldered people.

The lapels of a jacket should frame the face and allow your neck to have length. The most important space in a jacket scenario is the one between the chin and the top button. The longer this line is, the stronger the vertical will seem. The only exception to this rule is military-style jackets that feature metal buttons spaced, ladder-like, all through the centre front and create a vertical from hip to chin.

one-button jacket   *two-button jacket*   *three-button jacket*

A jacket that has one button at the waist is going to throw a long, flattering vertical line through the torso and neck. This style will work well on most bodies, but particularly on people who are busty.

Two buttons at the waist area obviously creates a shorter vertical through the body, and a three-button jacket, which usually has the top button positioned at the bust, has a very short vertical indeed.

A three-button jacket is always going to be problematic for bustier women as it will be more restrictive where they need freedom of movement the most. And for those with minimal bust the danger is that you end up looking like a boy. I am not a fan of the three-button jacket at all. It can be good on people who have a small waist when broken up with a belt detail to enhance the area, but otherwise the overall shape is too boxy to carry off.

Breast pockets, safari style, only ever work on small-breasted women. And ditto for hip pockets. You can only have them if you can afford the extra weight at that part of the torso. Remember that the eye will linger there if you add detail.

The same principles apply to the double-breasted jacket. More restriction, fewer verticals, and the danger of looking like a brick. While two rows of buttons should serve as a helpful double vertical, the reality is that they create a strong square shape on the torso, widening the body just where you don't want it to. An exception is the pea coat, which is longer and flares outwards from the hip. This introduces more verticals so the squareness of the double buttoning is offset.

What you wear under a jacket will obviously have an effect, too. Keeping a clean space between jacket buttons and chin will be most lengthening. Breaking it with a knit may be necessary, but watch where that knit sits and the impact the line has on the neck length. A higher neckline on a knit means less vertical in the neck. **A lower neckline means more lovely verticals.** Complicating the picture with a shirt will eradicate the verticals, so I would seriously think it through before putting that look together.

Jacket length can be determined by the same principles as the bodice length in a frock. If you are long through the torso, the jacket should be cropped, bolero style, or at most hitting the hip bones. Keep it shorter to allow your legs to appear longer. And for those with a shorter torso, a slightly longer jacket will balance the body. The one-button jacket will be the best choice here, with the strong middle vertical helping out.

Longer jackets just don't work with dresses and skirts, conjuring up Melanie Griffith in *Working Girl* with all the tragic 1980s style lines that went along with that. Keep a jacket short or cropped with skirts, or, better still, ditch the jacket for a sweet coat the same length as the skirt. **A coat is always more flattering than a jacket** because it is longer, allowing the eye to travel without interruptions. A coat is best of all over a frock, a skirt or trousers.

Tops

All the same principles apply for tops as for jackets regarding lines and shapes for different bodies. Your main consideration to ensure a flattering outcome here is the fabric from which tops are made.

If you need to conceal lumps and bumps, stay with darker colours and heavier fabrics as they will be more forgiving than satins and sheers, which will only highlight the problem.

Peasant shapes are only for slim people or you will end up looking more Frau than Fraulein. These styles add so much bulk to the body. There is definitely an age limit with peasant shapes too, so go with the age-old rule: 'If you have already lived through the fashion, don't repeat it.' A better option to achieve a similar whimsical look is to use pintucking through a more fitted top, or just choose peasant-style sleeves in a more fitted top if you can afford the bulk in that area.

Knits, while we love them for their ease and comfort, can be tricky, as their end point can be problematic (this applies to any top). Those with fuller hips should avoid breaking the torso at its widest point.

raglan sleeves

And with longer torsos, look for knits that feature a boat neck as this strong horizontal will mitigate body length. Shorter torsos can look great in tunic-style longer knits over fitted trousers, or dark tights if you have the legs for it. Bustier types will do best in lighter-weight wrap cardigan-style knits, as the crossover diminishes the vast expanse of chest.

Polonecks are great for those with long necks, but really, really bad on those with short necks, who are much better off with a low scooping neckline or a deep V.

Another consideration with knits is the boxy factor. Be sure that you choose shapes that highlight your good curves or glide over your bad ones. Avoid super clingy knits unless you are rake thin, as indentations of bra straps and waistbands look hideous.

Dresses

Here is the best suggestion I can give you for daywear.

Wear a frock – the garment that evolved around our girlie body shapes.

Now I'm going to do the hard sell.

The reasons why a frock is everybody's best option:

* You only have to make one garment decision in the morning. That means one garment to iron. One drycleaning expense, and also more space in your wardrobe.

* You can more easily eradicate any unwanted horizontals that will strip height from you. There is no need for breaks at the waist or hips unless they are design lines that you want to have. This means a more successful vertical line to the face.

Mere Mortal Tip #10

THE FROCK ROCKS

* You can avoid defining your waist height, which is useful for people with shorter or longer torsos. Ditto for crotch height and longer torsos. No one ever needs to know where your legs start.

* You can play up your killer feature more efffectively as there is less going on around other parts of the body. Accessories chosen with intent replace the design lines you would be forced to incorporate with separates.

Fitting

If a garment that you try on in a shop is tight or restrictive in any area, *put it back*. It is much better to buy the next size up and have looser areas altered to fit. This is particularly important when buying jackets and shirts. They must fit comfortably across the shoulders and bust.

If shirts have buttons that are too granny or too hussy for you, put them back too. The buttons must fasten at exactly the right spot vertically, a few centimetres above the fullest part of the bust. You can move buttons slightly horizontally to make the fit more or less snug, but the vertical position is fixed.

Any seams that are twisted or puckered will always remain that way. Bias-cut skirts will always retain their undulating seams if that is how they are in the store as you try them on. This cannot be fixed with pressing.

Tight linings will always be problematic. The lining is actually meant to be a little larger than the exterior of the garment to allow for ease of movement of the body. If your trousers are pale in colour, do us all a favour and make sure they are lined.

The key to getting the perfect fit is to find a great alterations person who you can go to directly and make the changes from good buy to great buy.

Taking day to night

Most of us have an inkling as to how to transform from working girl to glamourpuss. Depending on whether you are going out for hipper-than-thou cocktails or a fine-dining experience, you need to choose your daytime pieces well in the first place.

The addition of metallics is a dead easy solution for anything revolving around denim as it gives a glamorous night-time edge to the versatility of jeans. You could also look at adding luxe textures such as velvets and satin trims to pieces that will work back with denim for evening. It shoes or It bags, whether the latest incarnation of designer glam or old favourites, can deliver the same instant update to evening.

Basic blacks are easily transformed with the addition of strong colour in accessories, such as belts, evening bags and heels. Also, adding deeper shimmer and smokiness to your makeup will create another aspect to the same outfit.

Taking a business suit into night can be simply done using more feminine fabric in the underneath pieces. Silk camis rather than sensible knits transform day to night in seconds. The use of colour can be powerful too, and choosing complementary opposites of hues will add another dimension. Pick the hue up in your shoes as well and you have changed the business look entirely.

Dresses are simple to transform as they are so feminine anyway. The addition of a push-up bra if you need it, the change of subtle day jewellery to something more sparkly, the addition of a killer coat and some glamorous high heels replacing your sensible day shoes and you are ready to go.

Shooting Star

The hat trick

Let's face it: fifty years ago the prospect of popping a divine creation on our heads and running off to the races for the day would have been a no-brainer. Our grandmothers knew a good hat from a bad one, and the rules regarding seasons and trimmings. They knew how to tilt a hat to flatter them and how to keep it on in gale-force fashion conditions.

And then the 1960s were born and millinery died. So a generation of us have grown up clueless, going to Ascot and Aintree in dreadful chookie hats or appearing like extras from *Four Weddings and a Funeral* – or worse, wearing straw in autumn and felt in spring.

The key principle to remember with hats is that you should never look like there is a party happening on top of your head. Simple really. But, once again, so many people get it so very wrong.

The Star Style principles are really important in this chapter as there is both a micro (facial) and macro (overall body) setting to consider to ensure balance, and to make the eye travel easily through the body to that hat. Which, when done well, is the perfect accessory to add height and to grandly take attention away from problematic areas of our bodies.

Mere Mortal Racing Rule #1

THINK OF THE HAT AS EMBELLISHMENT, PHYSICALLY REMOVED FROM YOUR CLOTHING

You will learn to *love* a hat. It's like having a really gorgeous best friend that everyone tends to look at, only it's on your head and all the attention is yours.

The golden rules are the following.

When you wear a hat **the whole purpose of your frock needs to be as a support act for the hat**. The hat *is* the killer feature in a racing ensemble, and consequently the frock should be understated or hold more attention nearer the face and be very quiet down at the hem area. This ensures the eye is kept upwards and becomes embroiled in the beautiful millinery on display.

Of course, the Dot to Dot theory can also be applied if you are confident that you are not overcomplicating the look. Perhaps the handbag and shoes can have a colour or trimming in common with the hat. But beware the Jordan factor. If in doubt, keep it simple down there.

The right shoe will make or break your day. Remember to use Party Feet and think through the comfort factor. A seriously high heel is not really relevant anyway when the eye will be forced up to the face. If it's spring racing, you could be up for any kind of weather, and the most heartbreaking thing is to spend a fortune on party shoes and ruin them in the rain. There is nothing quite like the feeling of stiletto heels sinking into mud. Your cash is better spent north of your collarbone, and your feet just need to be present-able and comfortable.

The simple rules for millinery textiles:
* Autumn and winter racing are strictly felt, wool or cloth.
* Spring and summer racing require cinnemay, straw or cloth.
* Hats and headpieces are both appropriate for all seasons.

Feathers and flowers are also appropriate year round, but probably more favoured in the warmer seasons. For the cooler months textile trims are more popular with seasoned racegoers, as rain and feathers are not a good combination if you want to wear the hat more than once . . .

Shoes can be closed toe for all seasons, but you may prefer a slingback in the warmer months, if you have feet in tip-top condition. Strappy shoes and high-heeled sandals are fine for spring and summer, but not autumn and winter, when a closed-toe shoe with hosiery is required.

Mere Mortal Racing Rule #2

YOUR FEET ARE LESS
THAN SECOND FIDDLE

And on hosiery, the rules are likewise simple:

*   It is fine to wear hosiery with closed-toe shoes.

*   It is fine to *not* wear hosiery with closed-toe shoes.

*   It is *never* fine to wear hosiery with open-toe shoes.

The guideline used to be to match your hat with your shoes and handbag. This can still be relevant if you are deliberately using Dot to Dot to make your outfit work. Otherwise, keep the feet understated and your handbag small and well-positioned. Keep it in mind, too, that clutch bags are very tedious when trying to balance a glass of champagne, a race book and binoculars. Go for a handbag or shoulder bag, depending on your body shape.

Dresses or suits are both appropriate for the races. If the weather is looking suspicious, make sure you bring a wrap or, better still, a jacket. I don't want to have to point out the obvious, but this is an outdoor sport we are talking about. *Factor in the weather.* You don't want to spend the day shivering and trying to look fabulous in spite of the cold.

Frocks are very popular for racing. The rules are subtle here, with old-school racegoers frowning upon bare shoulders and a cocktail style of dressing. Sequins and shiny textures are not really appropriate for the races, but have crept into the scene anyway. The best way to approach it is to aim for somewhere between wedding guest and cocktail party, erring on the side of wedding guest. Remember, your frock is the sideshow to your hat, so if there is too much going on with the dress, the hat will not have the same impact. The best dresses for the races are simple shapes that are understated in embellishment.

Mere Mortal Racing Rule #3

HAT SIZE AND COLOUR ARE USED TO BALANCE FACE SHAPE

A larger face is complemented by a broader shaped hat, and darker hues are much more flattering than paler ones. Keep ornamentation such as flowers and feathers to a minimum, as the area should be subtly highlighted but not over-dramatised. You don't want to create a much larger area than is desirable. This is particularly relevant if you choose to wear a pale-coloured hat. Keep it simple. And this might be where you would use Dot to Dot theory in a racing outfit to move the eye upwards.

If you have a small face, you will be lost in a wide-brimmed hat, no matter how fashion-forward it may be this season. Small faces are best suited to stronger hues or paler tones, rather than dark shades, as these colours diminish the area, as you already know.

Try cocktail pieces, fascinators, beret shapes or whimsies to open up the area and add interest without you becoming lost in volume. You are blessed with the option of using bright colours as accents, and this is really helpful to keep the eye up and focused away from any troubles down below.

Securing your headpiece

Secure your hat using bobby pins and the hat elastic at the rear. If the weather is looking challenging, the Wardrobe Mistress's trick to secure headpieces is to purchase some *roulet tape*, also called buttonhole braid, which you will find in haberdashery stores. It's usually used for those gowns with zillions of little buttons running along a closure. It comes in black or white. If you have dark hair buy the black. White braid can be lightly sponged with some foundation to take it closer in colour to blonde tones. I sew or glue the braid around the inside edge of the headpiece and then position as many bobby pins in the braid as required to keep the piece in place.

The critical factor, though, is to *avoid having super-clean slippery hair*. Work out where exactly the piece will be placed and then have your hairdresser create what I call a 'nest', which has strong hairspray and teasing at the area your headpiece will be placed, making it easier to position the bobby pins and keep the piece in place through hell or high water. Or through too many champagnes, for that matter. It adds a new dimension to the term 'hat hair', doesn't it?

Smaller headpieces are often attached to Alice bands, which can be good for those who don't get blinding headaches from them (like me). But generally they are fixed to cocktail bases with slide combs or clips, which need help staying put.

When choosing a position for your headpiece, please remember which side of your face you favour. If you are unsure, spend some quality time alone with a mirror and look at how you pose for photos. Or look back through your albums.

Your headpiece or hat should be positioned on the side away from camera if you intend to take pictures, and it should never, ever, ever be front and centre on your head. Or I will personally seek you out and lecture you, I promise. A dramatic tilt downwards in the direction of your less favoured side will be complementary. This is the side that should have any ornamentation if you are using it. The detailing should run to the back of the head. No fringes of feathers please.

Remember that a diagonal line is always more flattering than a horizontal, and the tilt of a hat brim is an easy way to include one.

Hat pins are gorgeous but are really just ornamentation, so don't count on them. Rely on hairspray and bobby pins instead.

You can keep the inside head-band area of a hat clean of makeup by sticking a strip of Leukopore tape into the hat. It is comfortable and just peels away, so there are no makeup stains on the ribbon or headlining. This is a good tip if you are borrowing a friend's hat and wish to stay on her good side.

Remember, it's *One* Killer Feature. Your jewellery should never be in competition with your millinery. Stick to simple hoops or small diamond studs or whatever you fancy. Discretion is the key. And really think about whether you need a necklace. My guess is you probably don't. Choose jewellery logically.

Mere Mortal Racing Rule #4
SIMPLIFY YOUR JEWELLERY

If you choose to wear a smaller headpiece rather than a hat, you can look for inspiration from Hollywood movie stars from days gone by for your makeup. Think back to which star you are, and look at the millinery and makeup styles of that time. Statement lush lips, a perfect brow and a subdued eye can be very glamorous and enhance the overall look of a retro star. A wide-eyed natural look with a floppy wide-brimmed hat can work for hippy deluxe stars.

Choose hues that complement both the headpiece and your colouring, and if in doubt always go with warm neutrals as it is hard to go wrong with these. Once again, remember, your One Killer Feature is your hat in this instance. My theory about makeup has always been: present but not overpowering.

Mere Mortal Racing Rule #5
MAKE YOUR MAKEUP WORK

A wider-brimmed hat may call for slightly stronger makeup to balance it. This is where a smokier or more shimmery eye could work. Play around with your makeup beforehand and take lots of trial pictures wearing your hat so you can see where the balance of millinery and makeup will lie.

Shadows from brims will have an effect on your overall look, so what you think is right may be, in reality, way too dark. And remember that by the end of the day you will prefer it if you don't look like a panda. Enough said.

Two last tips: remember that there is a lot of social kissing, brim clashing and champagne drinking to be done, so an investment in a stay-put lipstick is worthwhile for the races. Colouring in the lip area with a lipliner rather than lipstick is also good as a stay-put solution. And choose a base with sunscreen in it so you don't get fried.

Starry, Starry Night

The beauty of eveningwear

Here is a big statement:

It's actually much easier to get eveningwear right than daywear.

I can imagine you shaking your head in disbelief, but it's true. While daywear has many dress codes imposed upon it, and requires an element of practicality, eveningwear has only one purpose. With daywear, you expect to be able to make separates work back to other pieces and force a versatility on every garment. There is a lot of pressure to get the bang for the buck with daywear. But not eveningwear. It just needs to look sensational. And it's unlikely that you will expect to wear an evening gown more than a few times, because of the '*I can't wear that. They have already seen me in it!*' factor.

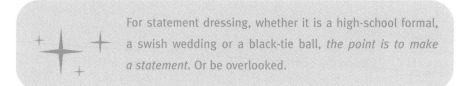

For statement dressing, whether it is a high-school formal, a swish wedding or a black-tie ball, *the point is to make a statement*. Or be overlooked.

Bodice, sleeves and neckline definition are crucial to creating the most flattering frocks. The subtle nuances of under-bust gathering, darts and drapes can throw the eye in one direction or another like sharp little arrows. Keep in mind where you want the arrows pointing, whether it's a Dot to Dot scenario or a straight-up-and-down motion. If you need clarification on any of the shapes mentioned in this chapter, check out the designs in chapter 9, Star Scape (the Look Book), which are there to guide you.

If you are shopping for an event, the top section of the outfit is most likely be captured in photographs as well, given that lots of pictures are tight shots. So keep this in mind. It is the last significant part of the dress before the viewer is looking into your eyes and therefore *critical* in a photo.

It's all about being very clear on your One Killer Feature again, and playing it up while diminishing your enemies. Special fabric treatments, beading, embellishment and texture can be used so effectively to carve out a new body. Stars have racks of clothing to choose from when they hit the red carpet, so believe me, the process they go through is much like this one, sifting through the options and working out which dress highlights their best assets. The dress doesn't appear by magic.

Getting the fabric right

The basic rules regarding fabrics are:

* Shiny fabrics increase the body area. Use them purposefully.
* Matte fabrics are more slimming.
* Velvets don't translate photographically in white but can look luscious in colours and in black.
* Laces are generally matte, but the size of the floral embellishment can act in a similar way to prints.
* Busy laces need thoughtful placement so they enhance your features, without adding to your bulk.
* Knits can be very flattering as they drape so beautifully.
* Clingy jerseys can look a bit trashy, so carefully think through the design lines and the underwear you are going to wear.

A few thoughts on colour

Colour has an important role to play in eveningwear. The level of 'Hello, look at me!' is amplified with its use. A simple, elegant design in black can have a whole lot of sass when made in red.

There is also the Re-wear Factor to consider. A black dress will have a better chance of coming out of the wardrobe a few more times before it is fashionably retired. A strong print or colour will automatically be labelled *that dress*, and probably not leave your home more than a couple of times. If you are going to spend a small fortune on a gown, decide initially what the Re-wear Factor needs to be. Be confident about that before you choose a colour.

If you are a wedding guest, avoid wearing white or creamy hues as it is just plain bad manners. Black is absolutely fine.

For evening it is great to break a black outfit with shoes and accessories that are metallic or coloured. This gives the outfit some joy and the eye the chance to play Dot to Dot.

Putting your One Killer Feature to work

By knowing what colours you want, and simplifying your design lines with the knowledge of what styles work on you, you are already halfway to never being challenged and intimidated by eveningwear again. It's important to keep focused. We tend to gravitate like magpies towards sparkly treatments and shiny fabrics as these are 'supposed' to be what p.m. dressing is all about. I say it's all about the maximum exposure of your killer feature and the confidence with which you wear the outfit. And some very good underwear to make your killer feature look even better.

Killer Feature: legs galore

If your killer feature is your legs then look at a **front split** in an evening gown. Consider the height of the split because the optical illusion you will create by going 5 centimetres in one direction or another can elongate you significantly. Or not. If modesty is an issue for you, really consider your underwear, as there are lots of products that will keep you nice and let you have legs galore. No commando style here, ladies, please.

When you are playing with your paper doll, experiment with the front split. Higher or lower with that split, more to the side or more central. Straight to the floor or curved slightly around to the hem. It's about the proportion of split length in relation to total body height to trick the eye into believing you have Legs Eleven.

Make sure you choose the side of your split according to how you naturally pose for photographs. It sounds curious but most people have a preferred side of their face and stand, pageant style, with one hip relaxed. Your split should be on the side that has the most leg visibility to use the optical illusion best.

The beauty of a front split is that it gives the world the opportunity to acknowledge your shoes, on which you have probably spent a small fortune. Have a look at every red carpet picture and you will see this principle played out over and over again.

If your evening gown has a one-shoulder feature (if the fickle winds of the fashion Gods are blowing in that direction at the time), consider a split on the same side as the shoulder detail. This will create Highway One right up from your pretty feet, through the body and to your face. Bingo.

A front split can be a bit like a Get Out of Jail Free card, in that it gives such a strong vertical aspect to the frock that you can get away with more neckline options and still achieve your glamazon status. So if it works for your shape then you have an easier path.

Great legs can be shown off wearing a shorter dress and higher heels, which accentuates the calf muscles. The best length is always the narrowest point just over or just under the knee. Never break the leg at its widest point.

You must remember: *A super-short skirt is not your friend.* Unless you are off to the MTV Awards or hip young things' equivalent, you will look trashy.

Also, a side seam split is not your friend. It will make your hips appear lopsided and create thigh horizontals even if you have great legs. If you don't believe me, just watch the Big Band scene from *Xanadu* and see what the skirts do to the dancers' bodies. Ghastly. If you can't stand the thought of watching *Xanadu* then just trust me.

Killer Feature: great hips and thighs

A style that is very popular at the moment is the classic Hollywood mermaid-style skirt. This will be really flattering on you as there are no dangerous curves to accentuate the horizontals so the eye can move easily towards the face. An even better version features the train at the back, which adds more verticals into the picture.

The position from which the sweep outwards to the floor starts needs careful consideration. Looking at your paper doll, find the point above the knee where the horizontal is still greater than the waist horizontal. This is where the sweep to the floor should start. The waist is still given the opportunity to be the narrowest horizontal this way, so you will look even slimmer.

If you wear a body shaper, your waist will be diminished and your hips and thighs become doubly as effective as a killer feature.

*mermaid-style
skirts: ensure
the waist is still
the narrowist
horizontal*

Other skirt shapes that will work for you are long and straight with a back split, slightly flared 1930s styles and bias-cut A-lines. Choose fabrics that glide over the hips as you can afford to do this. You can also afford shiny textures like satins and jerseys in the skirt area.

Killer Feature: smaller waist

If your hips are bigger than your bust, and your waist is your killer feature, you could look at A-line shaped skirts, huge 1950s New Look skirts or, in eveningwear, a full-blown meringue. Yes, indeed, there is a legitimate reason to wear a meringue if you really want to play the full fairy princess role. But please, for the sake of the rest of the world refer to inspirational gowns worn by Grace Kelly and Audrey Hepburn, even Queen Elizabeth II in her younger years. Not Jordan.

I mentioned on page 6 that there was a way around having hips like a small planet, and the full skirt certainly hides a multitude of sins. I made a gown once for a client who was seriously gorgeous, had a tiny waist but quite short legs, and the widest hips you could imagine. Her full hip measurement was 115 centimetres compared to a 64-centimetre waist, which is out of hand. In her 1950s inspired gown, with the swishy skirt and lots of petticoats, no one was any the wiser. Her tiny waist was highlighted with an upwards-moving band to give more length to her legs, and her hip size became irrelevant under the full skirt.

For a full skirt that is hiding large hips the logic is this: if we assume the easiest way for the eye to travel, given a wider hip than waist and bust, is triangular from the floor, then anything that reinforces that movement is a bonus. The best scenario here is to break the gown at the middle, using the thrust of the upwards-pointing triangle on the lower part of the body to direct the eye to the waist.

A strong upwards-pointing triangle can assist the vertical lines. It moves the eye upwards towards its point. This is what you want to find in a garment.

*a strong
upwards-
pointing
triangle
diminishes
larger hips*

Sometimes the point of the perceived triangle can be the waist. Sometimes it is the under-bust and sometimes even the neck. But the eye is moving upwards and that is what is important.

Ideally, smaller triangles that may exist between the shoulders and the middle of the body should also be there to highlight a narrow part of the body. This can be the waist, ribcage or high hip.

The strong horizontal break at the smallest part of the torso distracts from the comparatively larger hip area. And as the bust is not problematic here, you would find the gown balances well.

Having a small waist is a blessing, but it has to be shown to be small in comparison to something. So highlighting the area with a band or belt or even carefully placed embellishment like a brooch will force the eye to rest there and take in its wonder. Aim for the suggested small triangle of upper torso over a larger triangle with the two points meeting at the waist

If you wear a cincher, your small waist will become a tiny one and doubly as effective as a killer feature.

Killer Feature: great back

In eveningwear, the best look for a low back for *anyone* is a V shape. This offers lots of skin but lots of vertical motion too, and takes the eye to a full horizontal line across the back of the shoulders, making the waist appear smaller. Don't go too low as you will be concerned all evening about just how much of your bottom is on show when you are seated, and underwear issues also abound if the depth goes too far. Exposing the skin just to the bottom of the ribcage is very flattering as it allows the perceived verticals through the skirt area to be longer than if you choose to go very low cut at the back.

*the longer the
skirt triangle
in a low back
dress, the
stronger the
vertical*

If it works for your hip dimensions, an A-line or mermaid skirt will be the most flattering combination with the V back, as the points of the two triangular shapes will meet at the waist, hourglass style, and slim you down to almost nothing.

If you have a low-back dress, it's going to be a bit of overkill having a back skirt split as well. Theoretically it will give more verticals in the gown, which is good, but it could look a little trashy, which is bad. And, remember, never have a low back and a low front in the same gown. That is called overkill.

I am also a firm believer in having your hair up with a low-back frock. Otherwise you waste your best feature by covering it with flowing locks, making the whole exercise futile.

When you consider back straps, look at the strong lines they are creating.

> The wider the space across your shoulder blades,
> the thinner your waist will be perceived to be.

If you wear a cincher and a dress with a low-cut back, your waist will be diminished and your exposed back will be doubly as effective as a killer feature.

Killer Feature: great bust

They say, 'If you've got them, flaunt them', and this is particularly true of a killer bust. This doesn't mean that you have to channel Pamela, but certainly enlisting the support of a good push-up bra will work wonders. Embellishment at the bust is so helpful with the vertical aspects of an outfit too, as the attention is up at the top part of your body and close to the face.

Remember: the quieter the rest of your dress is,
the more effective the bust detail.

The most flattering halter, if you're that way inclined, is the bra or bikini-shaped cups that come from a pronounced under-bust seam. A bikini-style top is more flattering to the waist with vertical straps, though, rather than halter ones, as the verticals are stronger. The shoulders also read straighter with this line. Some girls just love a halter, though, and that's fine. The halter option adds perceived volume to the bust because the downwards sloping lines imply a stronger horizontal across the chest.

vertical straps, widely spaced   *vertical straps, closely spaced*   *halter straps*

A deep-plunging V-style halter (think Mariah Carey) is a good option if you need to lengthen a short body. A covered shoulder area that features a deep V plunge will help a longer torso seem shorter as there is less of an expanse of skin above the bust to break the body.

If strapless is your thing, consider a sweetheart dip at the centre front as this opens up the area and adds a nice vertical hint. You can afford to go to town with draping, ruching, beading and other embellishment at the bust if it's your killer feature.

If you do choose strapless, make sure you can include twice your neck length between the chin and bodice. This helps to balance the strong horizontal of your shoulders with a lovely long neck. An easy way to achieve the length through the décolletage is to use a sweetheart-shaped bodice rather than one that just cuts across the bust. There is an implied vertical this way and you are not revealing too much actual breast.

A good male friend of mine has made it very clear that what boys are looking for in Killer Breasts is what he calls 'side nork'. Elegant. Apparently, this little glimpse of side bust carries more weight with the lads than traditional centre cleavage. It would only make an appearance with halter-necks that scoop low to the sides of the dress. So if it's a boy you are hoping to impress, rather than your female fashionista buddies, that's your hot tip.

Killer Feature: great shoulders and neck

Athletic-cut necklines are a good choice to show off a great neck and shoulder area. In order to make sure that your waist doesn't become the wider horizontal with this design, it is good to use embellishment at the neck edge to keep the eye high.

Another neckline that looks great with this killer feature is the boat shape, which sits just on the collar bone. There is a lower version, too, which is a bit like a strapless bodice, only it continues over the bicep. Audrey Hepburn was often photographed in this elegant neckline, and it framed her face beautifully. A statement necklace would really work in this scenario.

Strapless is a good choice too because there is no option but to behold the beautiful neck. Perhaps minimise the embellishment at the bust, though, and accessorise with jewellery to send the eye to the neck.

athletic-cut necklines enhance the neck and shoulders

Diminishing the enemies

If you use shape, texture and colour logically, the business of diminishing the enemies should be straightforward. There is a mantra to remember when thinking about Worst Enemies. Matte, matte, matte; dark, dark, dark. How easy is that? Good-quality fabrics will glide over the body and will be assisted by a decent lining. It's important to never have tightness around the Worst Enemies as this pulls the eye back towards them.

The bust v. hip scenario

If your bust is not wider than your hips, you can afford to use a contrast fabric or texture, shine or embellishment in eveningwear through the upper part of your frock. This can have two bonuses. Firstly, it acts as a highlight towards the top of the body, giving you more height. And also, if you use a darker or matte fabric for the skirt then it will make the body slimmer as well. Bingo.

If your bust is wider than your hips, you should try to balance the triangles of bodice and skirt with a fuller skirt that glides over the hips. This will carve out a smaller waist. The better neckline in this scenario is a V shape as it forces a vertical into the fuller bust and hints at a smaller waist.

Long v. short torso

If you have a good bust but a long torso, a strapless dress is a good basic idea for you to work with because it will shorten your trunk slightly with the absence of vertical lines in the way of straps. Embellishment at the bust could work too unless you are quite busty.

If you have a shorter torso, think about how you keep the eye moving. Statement earrings or embellishment at the top edge of a frock are choices to consider. You can interfere with the strapless line by making it more sweetheart in cut, or even quite angular so that it's more in the shape of an M. This forces the eye up and down, which is going to be of more help than just allowing it to go straight across.

You can interfere with the strapless bodice line, breaking it with a feature trim, like our grannies used to do with a corsage or brooch. And, more recently, like designers have done with stiffened bows, etc. Another addition could be V straps from the centre of the bust.

Arm anxiety

While we are on this area of skin across the upper chest, let's look at the use of wraps and stoles for those who have arm anxiety.

The wider you can let your wrap sit across the shoulders, or preferably slightly off the shoulders, the better you will look. Wearing a wrap close to the neck has a touch of Granny about it and doesn't deliver as strong a shoulder horizontal.

And, luckily for those of us with arm anxiety, eveningwear is coming back to embracing the sleeve. Princess Mary of Denmark got it so right with her wedding dress, whereas Princess Fergie didn't. A sleeve in an evening gown should be cut close to the arm and highly pitched under the armpit, and shouldn't command attention and draw the eye horizontally around the bodice.

let your wrap sit across the shoulders

If you have slimmer hips, bell sleeves and tulip sleeves can be worn. The fullness of the sleeve will fall at an area that can take that extra volume.

A small puff sleeve or high tulip shape is better for those with smaller busts and broader hips.

A slim three-quarter-length sleeve flatters any body shape, and embellishment with ornate buttons etc. could be used unless hips are a problem.

Just remember that once you have decided on an evening gown style, you have to find the corsetry that will make you look even better. Refer to chapter 7 for more detail.

The vertically challenged

The best possible length for a short person's evening gown is full length. If you can afford a front split then do it. The fewer horizontal lines the better. And as much detail as you can create should be at the top of the gown.

The willowy

Reduce your perceived height with as many horizontal breaks as you can put into the gown. Choose a fuller skirt to create a strong horizontal at the hem, and ballerina length rather than full length will help you. Add dramatic interest at the bodice with ruching or draping to keep the eye busy and centred low. A personal issue I have with straight skirts on taller women is when they try to wear a full-length skirt and pretend it actually is a cocktail length. Yes, height is a good thing, but make sure your skirt length clearly shows a great calf muscle rather than saying 'I'm too tall to wear this full-length dress properly.' Make the skirt length intentional.

Having a gown made

At this stage you will be able to walk into any eveningwear store and choose *purposefully* which dress is going to look good on you. But a much better option, if you have the time and can afford to do so, is to have your gown made. For brides, www.sewdirect.com and www.macculloch.com (see chapter 10) have extensive lists of good dressmakers who specialise in bridal. This means that they can handle the luxury fabrics and trims of eveningwear easily and create something unique for you. Another way to find a good one is to visit a quality fabric store and ask who they can recommend. They will usually have some names to refer you to.

Commercial patterns are so good these days, and you will find designs very close to what you are looking for in the collections from Vogue, McCall's, Simplicity, etc. It is possible, too, to Frankenstein the bodice of one pattern with the skirt of another, but discuss this with the dressmaker in case there are technical limitations. Using a blend of commercial patterns cuts down the cost, as there is less in the way of pattern-making time needed to create the frock. I do this all the time for red carpet frocks and bridal gowns that I design, and get great results.

There is a world of difference in having a gown made. Length measurements, like front splits, for example, can be made to flatter *you*. Not just a generic stab in the dark, the measurement will be exactly what you need. Bodices can be cut to fit your dimensions exactly, and work brilliantly over your well-chosen corsetry. In-between sizes are no longer an issue. If you are a size 8 up top and a size 14 down below, this can be managed better in a made-to-measure gown.

If your budget will stretch to it and the occasion demands it, do consider this option. You will feel like a million dollars and, in addition, you will certainly not have the worry of running into someone else in your dress.

6

Wish Upon
a Star

Happy ever after

You're only a bride once. Actually, you're only a *Bridezilla* once. Hopefully you marry the right man the first time and never have to put your friends and family through the ordeal of a second trip down the aisle. While second-time brides usually know themselves and their tastes better (which is why they divorced in the first place), the pressure is still very strong to Get It Right.

Just because you are getting married, it doesn't mean that you have to lose all sense of reason and wear something that will make you cringe in years to come. And just because you are The Bride, it doesn't mean that you get to frighten your groom with alarming choices of frock, hair and makeup. You get years to alarm him after you have signed the papers. You need to find a way to be The Bride and still be yourself. A gorgeous, more beautiful than any other day of your life version of yourself.

When choosing a gown, don't make a decision based on wearing it again after the wedding. You won't. I have, in all my years of working on brides, only known one who did indeed wear her dress again.

All the same principles apply regarding choosing a design that works for your body shape, but there is one overriding factor to deal with.

White

Whether it's ivory, cream, silver, magnolia, buttercream or palest icy pink, the fact remains that a block of a super-pale hue will definitely add a size to your frame. So any design that was borderline before is now under serious scrutiny.

There are so many versions of white. Synthetic whites tend to throw off a hard blue tinge that you will not find with silks. True white is only found in synthetics, as nature doesn't create it quite that way. It can be hard to wear, and is probably better suited to people with classic blue-based English rose complexions.

There is more reason than ever to keep a wedding gown simple. Beading, ornate laces and trims just add bulk to the overall body of the frock, and kilos to your frame. The key words to keep in your mind are: Clean. Classic. Classy. Rather than Jordan, think Carolyn Bessette-Kennedy. Rather than Jessica Simpson think Nicole Kidman. You get the picture.

It is crucial that, after you decide which style of dress you would like, you do all fittings with the right bridal corsetry. *Find the underwear first*. Just like building a house, you start with the foundations and build up from there.

> Take a step back from being The Bride and
> really look at dress design.

The detailing at the front of the dress needs to be scrutinised, particularly in the top 40 centimetres. While there will be full-length shots taken, the majority of wedding photos are mid close-ups. Make sure that all design lines in the bodice work with you, not against you. All draping, tucks and darting should be there as specific lines that send the eye in the appropriate direction. Your One Killer Feature has to be clearly enhanced and your Worst Enemies should be beaten.

Pay special attention to the back of the gown. This is what your guests will be looking at as you gaze lovingly into the eyes of your groom. If there is a zip closure at the centre back, is it an ugly zip? Is it an invisible zip? Are there feature buttons creating a vertical aspect through the gown? If the back of the dress has to be plain, perhaps consider a V rear neckline or a cascade of fabric from the waist. Something to give you a vertical, if that's what you need. And while a train isn't for everyone, it is an excellent lengthening design tool worth considering if you are looking for more verticals.

Getting the fabric right (again)

When choosing fabrics, remember that:

* Shine, such as you will find in satins, taffetas, metallics and all-over beaded materials, will make the body area larger. Use them purposefully.
* Matte, like crepe de chine, georgette and satin-back crepe, is more slimming. Velvets, while lovely to the touch, don't translate photographically in white, so while they are expensive they may not be a wise choice.
* Laces are generally matte, but the size of the floral embellishment can act in a similar way to prints. There are perfectly lovely laces for £20 per metre and exquisite laces for £200 per metre, so make sure you are clear about what you want, and if a designer will not accommodate your budget then shop around. The mark-up on laces for bridalwear is quite a business.
* A busy lace can increase perceived mass, and a larger design needs careful placement. Beaded laces require critical placement so they enhance your features, not add to your bulk.
* Jerseys can be very flattering as they drape so beautifully, but clingy dresses can look a bit trashy, so think carefully.

The veil

Another design tool you might choose to use is the bridal veil. A very traditional accessory, they may not be the best idea for very modern-looking gowns, but are still very popular. While I must say I am not a fan, to many they put the Fairy into Fairy Princess. The tiara at the top could be a Dot to Dot final point, so if you are wearing a veil, remember that.

tiered veil and cascading square veil

The right veil can act as a strong vertical. The length is important, though, as you want to avoid a break in the overall shape, which would result in an unwanted horizontal line.

As a rule of thumb, the leaner the silhouette of the gown, the longer the veil should be. A cascading square-shaped veil is good because it incorporates some verticals into the picture; a good choice for slim gowns. It drapes in a diamond shape on the bias, and has a vertically cascading zigzag affect. A satin binding on this shape can create an interesting highlight, which might also be of use.

The fuller the skirt is, the more layers of tulle you can incorporate into the veil. Puffy skirt means puffy veil. And if you do choose the double puff, consider your hairstyle well, because having your hair up or back may the best option for creating an oasis within the puff. Puffy hair is probably not a good idea.

A fingertip-length veil can be a good choice for dresses like Leah Wood's, a fairly plain gown with much of the detail incorporated into the antique lace veil. Again, the length sends the vertical message and prevents breaks in the design.

It is important to remember that if you intend to wear a full-length veil, it is at least thirty centimetres longer than the train in the dress. It should also echo the shape of the train. If the gown is only to the floor, then the veil can either be floor length as well, or you could let it trail for a metre or so behind the dress.

One point about floor-length dresses is this. They should be just that. Floor length. Make sure when you are in fittings that you wear the actual shoes you will wear on the big day, and that the skirt is no more than one centimetre off the floor.

Wear your shoes for half an hour every day of the week leading up to the wedding so they will be worn in appropriately. And invest in Party Feet.

Headpieces

The recent trend back towards cocktail and whimsy shapes, sometimes with feathers or veiling for weddings, is very sweet and very effective.

Rather than having metres of tulle draped around your face, the careful placement of a headpiece can be a flattering option that draws the eye up to the head immediately. The styles of dress these work with are more the retro slimmer shapes or Dior New Look styles that call for a vintage accessory, so if you are going meringue or very full through a *modern* skirt, a beautiful single fresh flower might be a better style option. Either way, this is a great tool for adding height to an outfit and slimming the body as a result.

As with racing wear, experiment with the best side of the face on which to wear it. The side facing away from camera is usually best, and in a wedding scenario that means talking to your celebrant about who is standing where. The same principle applies to hairstyles too. You don't want an album of hair shots, no matter how great your do is.

Take your headpiece or flower to your hairdresser so that you can both work with it to find its best position.

Hair and makeup

Here's a thought. What about having a little think about what the groom likes? I know it's a crazy idea, as it's widely known that grooms are to have *no* opinions on the planning of the big day, but I have found that most men are quite specific about hairstyles they like on their brides.

And while lots of brides choose the up do, lots of men prefer hair to be out, and wonder if the vision in white is really the same woman they proposed to.

So I beg you. Have the conversation. You are marrying *him*. If it turns out that he doesn't have an opinion, well then, just go ahead and have whatever do takes your fancy; but if he does love your hair in a certain way, then try to find a compromise – the first of many, by the way – and talk to your hairdresser about a style that will work for both of you, and your dress. Having your hair clear of your neck, whether as an up do or a half-up do, will give a clean vertical through the neck, so it is worth discussing that with your hairdresser.

And on that. Book a good hairdresser and makeup artist as soon as you set the date. Good ones book up months in advance and you can't afford to not have a good glamour team working on you. Bridal website www.hitched.co.uk has many names on its books and you can see at a glance what kind of work different stylists do. The bridesmaids and mothers can sort themselves out later, but you must book the star of the show in early.

And please spend the extra money and have a trial. The more photos you have for the stylists to refer to, the better your chances of getting something you like. Be clear about how much makeup is enough makeup, and don't believe everything you hear about needing a thick base for photographs. It just isn't true. If you are not the type of person who likes to wear a face full of slap, and that's what you get bullied into, then you will be thinking about it the whole of your wedding day. Better to go light and natural-looking, and enjoy yourself.

Take pictures of the trial from every angle so you can be sure you are happy with the look. Ask the makeup artist to write the products down for you if you really love them, so you can add them to your own makeup kit. Sometimes a fresh set of professional eyes can do wonders for your day-to-day make up.

Spray tan is the natural enemy of the wedding gown. If you really, really must have one, book it early and check that there will be no rub-off on the gown. That is officially the trashiest wedding look possible. Double Bahamas is a look you want on the honeymoon, not on the wedding dress.

The bouquet

The bouquet will be in many of the photos and it has a role to play in the look of a wedding gown, too. Generally it sits front and centre of the photos. How will you make it work for you? Will the size and shape of the bouquet work with the gown's design lines?

Your height has a role to play in working out how long the arrangement should be. Experiment with garden foliage and a full-length mirror before making any serious commitments.

* A small, rounded posy bouquet will keep the waist area fairly even.

* A large, rounded posy bouquet will increase the waist area.

experiment before making a (bouquet) commitment

* A large triangular teardrop bouquet will increase the overall waist area, but its verticals at least will give some height as well.

* A sheath or armspray bouquet will have many more verticals and be the most flattering choice for many body shapes.

* Cascading, unstructured bouquets can be very pretty, but send the eye in many directions without purpose.

* A darker colour diverts attention and is more slimming than a paler bouquet, so consider this when choosing the flowers as well.

a darker coloured bouquet will make the waist look smaller

You will be wearing that bridal ensemble for up to twelve hours. So, try everything on and walk around in the ensemble for at least an hour one week before the wedding madness. You will then become aware of anything likely to annoy you on the big day. Labels that might need to be removed, earrings that are uncomfortable, a veil that is scratchy. Take photos and check every aspect one more time, before you put the gown away.

Jewellery

When in doubt, refer back to the Dot to Dot theory. If the jewellery has no purpose other than being pretty and desirable, then why do you intend to wear it?

Necklaces are the first things that I consider putting away. If you deliberately want to play up the neck area then that's fine. If there is *no* design reason to wear one then rethink it. More is definitely too much.

Perhaps a bracelet gives you better Dot to Dot. Perhaps your earrings are enough of a statement without the necklace.

You are a bride, not a Christmas tree.

If you are wearing a veil, consider wearing smaller earrings as the extra volume around the face can be a bit overwhelming with great dangling chandeliers as well. Remember: Clean. Classic. Classy. Save Beyoncé's earrings for the honeymoon.

THE BRIDAL SURVIVAL PACK

Here's what I always take along when I dress the bride. Or when I am the bride. Please understand I am not a chemist and I would never ever recommend that you take medication without a good chat to your doctor first. Also, you can buy tiny bottles from the chemist into which you can decant the liquid items below if you can't find sample sizes.

* 2 Panadol – for bridal headache
* 2 Feminax – for bridal 'OMG I can't believe I got my period today and I'm doubled over in pain!'
* 3 tampons – ditto above with a white frock in the equation
* 2 Piriton – for bridal hayfever from the bouquets you are allergic to
* 1 pocketpack of tissues
* Mints
* Dr Lipp balm (it's the only one that doesn't dry your lips out) and lipstick
* Mirrored powder compact
* Witch hazel for potential blemishes. I love witch hazel to bits.
* 2 individual eye drops

* Sample-sized tube of the moisturiser you use every day. This will help if your eye drops make your eye makeup run.

* Sample-sized bottle of the perfume you wear every day

* Tiny bottle of insect repellent if it's an outdoors affair

* Tube of antiseptic cream for potential insect bites

* 4 Tapeits

* 4 safety pins

* Needle, thread and tiny scissors

* Anti-static spray

* 2 plasters

* 4 hair pins if your hair is up

* Mini hairspray if you think you will need it

* Pocket-pack of Wet Ones

* White chalk

* Scholl Party Feet

* A change of shoes for later on in the night when you begin to feel like you want to sever your feet from your ankles.

After you have dressed, give the kit to your favourite aunt/sister/friend so she will feel needed. And believe me, she will be needed at some point during your big day.

Under the Stars

The miracle of underwear

Although much of this chapter can be applied to daywear, it's really dedicated to the important foundations to be worn under eveningwear and bridal gowns.

I know we have so much to thank the Women's Movement for, but whoever decided that the burning of bras was a good idea was a lunatic. Actually, whoever it was probably had no need for a drop-dead-gorgeous evening gown now that I think about it.

When you consider the corsetry that our grandmothers had to endure as part of the everyday routine of dressing, we really have it easy. These days we have our abs on the inside (go figure!) rather than depending on a girdle. We choose to buy our body-slimming foundations, whereas in a previous era they were de rigeur after the age of twenty. We are not thought of as brazen hussies if we are out without a petticoat, and bare legs are quite fine, thanks, Nanna. Which is all good.

Guess why they call it foundation wear?

Underwear is the basis, the starting point over which your frock will fall. Yes, we all know that a bit of boning in a strapless dress is helpful, and that a lining makes us feel a bit fancy-schmancy. But think about the difference of shaving 5 centimetres off your waist, or lifting your breasts 4 centimetres, or having a bottom that sits up high like you have been on the exercise bike all year. Most of us cannot afford to not be on very good terms with our favourite lingerie department.

A dress that looks good without the right underwear will look ten times better with it.

I want a waist like Grace Kelly

Having a defined waist helps to reinforce the design triangles that will support the shape of your dress. But even people with smaller waists can do with some support to flatten the natural roundness at the front of the tummy. Everyone stands straighter and taller with some structure around their midriff. Corsets and torsolettes are one way to achieve the wasp waist, but cinchers are another, and are less restrictive than their cousins in that they finish under the bust.

Don't choose your dress until you have chosen the Secret Weapons that will go under it.

Secret Weapon #1: The waist cincher.

These come in a few shapes. Basically they are a firm, wide band, sometimes with boning that cinches the waist, usually starting at the hipbone and finishing midway through the rib cage. They are available in G-string form, or to mid-thigh like a bicycle short, and also just as a band, unattached to a brief. Because they stop quite high the muffin-ery explosion is curtailed. With the cinchers that have a fairly normal brief attached, double check that there is no cutting VPL on show. Generally I steer people towards the G-string option or the full granny bike-short option to avoid this.

Normal girdles can slim your waist but push the rolls of lard out the top of the waist elastic, which is not good. Cinchers are best used if you are not intending to wear a bra with your gown, but want to be slimmer through the waist.

The best cinchers are:

*   Naomi and Nicole's High Waist Brief with Wonder Edge. There is no VPL with this particular cincher.

*   The Miraclesuit Waist Cincher, which has a hook and eye closure through the back.

*   Annette Power Curves Waist Cincher is similar but has the hook and eye closure through the front instead, which is much easier to work with.

*   And even better if you prefer your cincher with a higher-leg brief attached is Doreen Fashion's Shapewear 7 Waistnipper Brief, again with a front hook and eye closure strip.

*   Rago Thong Back Waist Cincher from Lady Grace.

*   The Miraclesuit Waist Extra Control High Waist Brief.

*   Figleaves' Annette Power Curves High Waist Firm Control Brief, which features a zip closure through the front, and an adjustable cotton crotch.

*   Figleaves' Annette Power Curves High Waist Firm Control Thong, a G-string cincher brief, with the same concealed zipper as its friend, above.

*   The Nancy Ganz Hi Waisted Belly Buster is really quite amazing.

*   Flexees Zipper High Waist Hi Cut Brief with a zipper front closure and serious control. This is from Lady Grace.

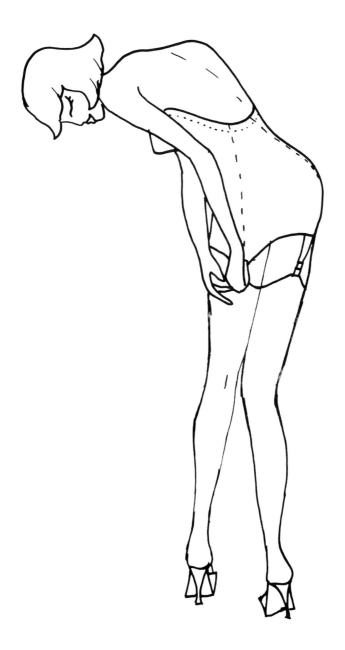

I want thighs like J Lo

Well, let's get one thing clear right now. Make sure you know exactly where your thigh shapers will end if you have any kind of leg split in a frock. Granny knickers are not to be seen in public. If you are wearing a split in the dress, you must try on potential underwear first and then proceed.

Secret Weapon #2: The thigh shaper

Try these ones to diminish your thighs:

* The Miraclesuit High Waist Thigh Slimmer.

* Naomi and Nicole's Light Control Thigh Slimmer with Wonder Edge.

* Nancy Ganz The Belly Band Bike Short.

* Nancy Ganz Body Slimmers Convertible Bust Shaping Bodyslip.

* Figleaves' Body Wrap Bra Slip is similar but has a strapless option.

Secret Weapon #3: The thigh and bottom shaper

Body Wrap make a product called Seamless Control Hi Waist Long Leg that looks like bike-short-length opaque pantyhose but basically trims you around the waist, hips and thighs to the knees and also lifts and supports your bottom. Amazing. It even has an open crotch for practicality. We're talking a reduction of 5cm at the waist and hips, which is a much better option than liposuction, I think. Perfect for gowns with a mermaid-skirt feature, as the underwear will be completely hidden. It takes a while to wriggle into it though so be prepared. All good things come to those who wait.

Secret Weapon #4: The thigh, bottom and waist shaper

Dangerous curves ahead. Figleaves have a suit called The Body Wrap Seamless Control Capri that has a very long leg, and also Wacoal's Try A Little Slenderness High Waist Panty, offers serious support for the tummy, hips and thighs and has the best name in this chapter. If your tummy is just fine there is a normal-waisted version too.

Secret Weapon #5: The bottom in a box

Sad, isn't it? Yes, there are girls out there with boy's bottoms. The answer to being a bit more Beyoncé and a bit less Beckham is Figleaves' Rago Padded Shaper Panty, and there is a longer-line version called Venus Padded Panty from Lady Grace which also has light shaping in the front tummy panel. The great names just keep coming don't you think? Both have removable pads and a tummy panel for light shaping. They give your evening gown a girlie bottom to sit over.

There is also the Just A Kiss Padded Shorty by Huit Lingerie available through Figleaves. These amazing underpants have technology imbedded in them that means that they become the Wonderbra equivalent for your derrière.

I want a bust like Salma Hayek

There are many issues to think about when trying to achieve the perfect bust. First of all, you need to take care of the skin at the decolletage. There are many beauty creams that offer firming and spot reduction; I'm not convinced they really deliver, but at least they rehydrate the skin (and that can only be a good thing). The next thing to consider is the best kind of support or enhancement for you. The bras listed in this section should cover most needs and help you find the best pieces for your particular bust. I do beg you, though, to keep a little separation between the breasts so that you avoid the classic Jessica Rabbit look of bosoms squished together which is trashy, trashy, trashy.

Secret Weapon #6: The push 'em up and push 'em out bra

Not such a secret anymore – there are so many push-up, padded and gravity-defying bras now that the small-busted among us can be confident we will be well looked after.

Lingerie stores are full of good push-up bras like the Elle MacPherson Intimates Double Skins Contour Bra and Lovable's Bodysilk Moulded Push Up Bra, two standouts.

The Wardrobe Mistress advises you against gel or water filled bras as the worry of wardrobe malfunctions should not be something that is on your mind when you are all glammed up.

Some of the finds from cyberspace are quite spectacular, and if nothing else it's amazing to trawl the websites and see just how much is now available to us courtesy of international shipping. Try these:

* Figleaves' Aubade Piraterie De L'Amour padded plunge bra. This has bonus removable va va voom pads.

* Victoria's Secret Very Sexy Plunge Strapless Convertible Bra allows you to position the straps in five different ways. The depth of plunge is pretty generous so if your dress has a deep neckline this is your bra.

* Victoria's Secret Very Sexy Secret Embrace Push Up Bra, which is seam-free and label-free and delivers quite a bust indeed.

* Victoria's Secret Very Sexy Extreme Plunge Push Up Bra, with graduated padding and a very deep front.

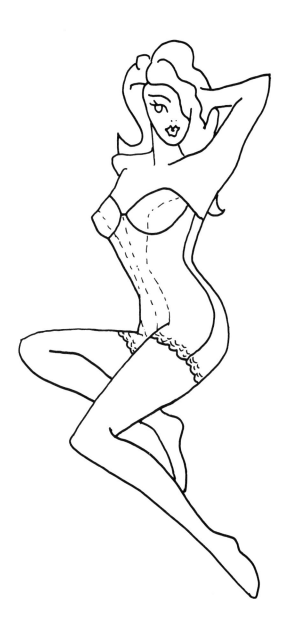

Secret Weapon #7: The minimiser bra

The Fayreform Underwired Minimizer Bra reduces bust projection, which can be useful if you want a smoother bustline. This is a very popular minimizer catering for a size range 32E to 40G.

Figleaves can despatch Wacoal Elegance Hidden Wire Minimizer Bra to you, which is a pretty bra. (For some reason, designers like to make ugly bras for women with large busts. It makes no sense to me!) This lovely one covers the size range 38C to 44G. There is also the Aviana Embroidered Underwire Minimizer from Figleaves, which promises a reduction of 3cm and reduces projection significantly. This one goes from 32D to 46H. That's some bra.

Secret Weapon #8: The extra special artillery

There are three bras that are so brilliant, they should be in the Underwire Hall of Fame.

The U Bra has the deepest plunge on the market. It even enables you to add more pads into little pockets to create more cleavage if you choose. The straps are convertible too so you can wear a variety of necklines with confidence and there are longer-line versions as well as bodysuits on the market. It is smart to actually go down a back size to maximize cleavage in the U Bra, but have a play and also look at the less expensive versions in department stores. There is also a version which has an inbuilt cincher so you can also define the waist. Brilliant. There is now no excuse for a bust problem with a deep neckline shape.

The Debenhams 5 Way Strap Convertible Bra is designed to run lower at the back. It can be strapless, or you can use the almost invisible straps under a gown, but the beauty of it is this. Most strapless bras run horizontally around the torso, making it hard to wear a dress with a low back. This one enables you to do just that with an extra strap that supports the bra towards the front.

Lauren Silva's Ultimo Miracle Backless Bodysuit is very plunging at the front and extremely low cut at the thong-shaped back, plus it has gel-filled bust inserts if you need them. Fantastic.

Here are some other ingenious bras for style solutions:

* Victoria's Secret Very Sexy 100 Way Convertible Bra, which is a feat of modern engineering and delivers a great cleavage. One hundred ways with a bra could be a continuing education course!

* Victoria's Secret Very Sexy Vertical Cup Convertible Bra, Very Sexy Secret Embrace Vertical Cup Bra, both of which feature cutaway cups and minimal coverage, a little like the U Bra, yet delivering amazing va-va-voom.

* Allure Lingerie padded push-up underwire bra, which is an adhesive strapless bra that can be reused with the extra adhesives in the package.

* Figleaves' The Natural Strapless and Backless Wing Bra. This is a deep-plunge miracle bra. With serious wire support underneath, this little wonder is ideal for a backless dress and a red-carpet winner.

* Also by Figleaves is the Fashion Forms Extreme Silicone Plunge Bra which has less plunge and a little more coverage. Then there is Useful Chick Stuff's amazing but weird stick on strapless bra, both ingenious adhesive products that keep you up and out there in backless dresses.

Boostits, the silicone inserts that come in full-cup and half-cup sizes, have a role to play as well in sculpting the perfect bust, especially if you are a member of the Itty Bitty Titty Committee, but it is much better to get the padding and support you need through structure. It's just one less thing to think about on your big night.

Secret Weapon #9: Corsets and torsolettes

These are great, although you do feel a bit like a stripper initially. They offer amazing support to a gown, can trim centimetres off your waist and force you stand with better posture. Avoid anything that is flimsy and probably designed for boudoir use only, as the whole point is to take advantage of boning and structure to make your dress look great.

There are so many available, but the basic one I love is the Vera Wang Enhancers Backless Bustier from Figleaves. It is smooth rather than lacy and has a good deep plunge, with moulded cups rather than seamed ones which is better under eveningwear. Also, Finelines Strapless Low Back Torsolette from Zodee is a favourite that I have used a million times for red carpet. I like to sew padding, like Fluffies, into the bottom of the cups for smaller-busted clients so that the natural bust sits on top. You can also use Breast Friends. This can add 5cm or so to the bust.

Finelines have recently released another legend, in the Refined Lines Collection.

It's called the Strapless Convertible Plunge Bustier and it offers a U bra depth of plunge in a corset form. This means that you have all the benefits of support and va-va-voom in a strapless outfit, with the added joy of plunge.

Lingerie Express has many corsets available for sizes right up to 42F, so there is definitely something there for all of us. The best one is the Tapestry Corset by Intimate Attitudes which laces up the back for a super-tight fit.

The Victoria Satin Corset from Glamour Corsets is a long-line design that flattens the hip area is that's what you are looking for. They make it right up to a size 20. There is also a shorter version, The Victoriana Satin Corset which still has the back lacing detail and metal boning, but finishes at the high hip.

Figleaves' Vollers Under-bust Corset is a fantastic boned creation that will shape an hourglass figure for you.

The Wardrobe Mistress advises sewing press studs onto the top edge of a corset and to the corresponding points on the gown so that the two never separate during the course of an evening. It is good to not have to think about whether your underwear is making a celebrity appearance.

When buying a corset, choose a size that is 5 to 8 centimetres smaller than your actual waist size so there is scope for cinching.

Our Grandmothers had it right all along, wearing foundations that set them up to seem to have much better shapes than was the reality. A dress that looks goes on you before the wonders of foundation wear will look amazing afterwards. Don't think for a minute that those red-carpet photos we all critique are perfect without these Secret Weapons. Those women are mortal too.

The last word is this, though. Beware the Bridget Jones giant underpants fiasco if you are intending to bring home Hugh Grant!

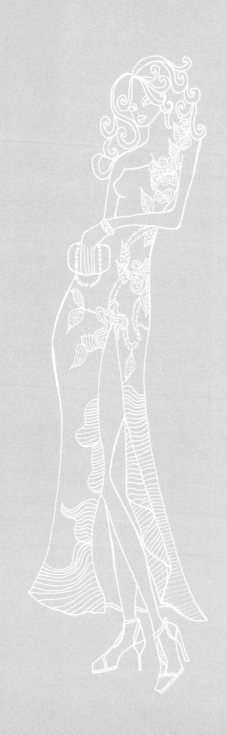

8

Twinkle, Twinkle

A sprinkling of sparklers

The Dot to Dot theory really comes into its own in this chapter. Accessories, particularly metallic ones such as jewellery, provide easy access points for the lazy eye, so you can use them to manipulate the flow of your outfit to flatter you.

You have to accessorise with intent.

Basically, if you can imagine a black head-to-toe outfit punctuated by silver crystal-encrusted slingbacks, a sparkly diamond ring and bracelet on the same hand and a pair of statement diamond earrings, you can imagine how easily the eye travels from one point to the next. You could replace the shoes with red suede pumps, the bracelet with a Fendi B bag and the earrings with a textured beret with the same result.

The important thing is to know what types of accessories are going to flatter you before you start to add them. On a micro level there is the face, and on a macro level there is the whole body.

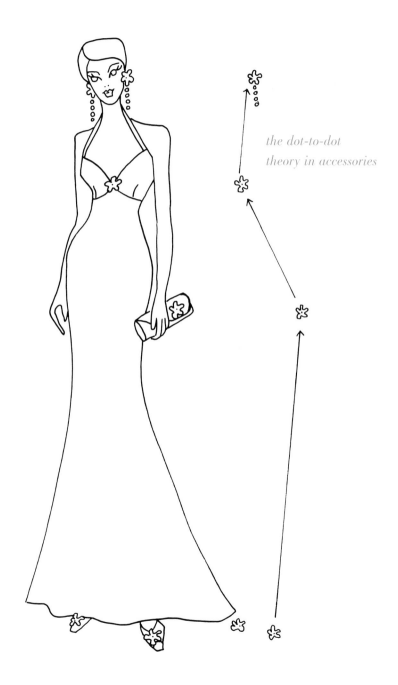

*the dot-to-dot
theory in accessories*

Star style: jewellery

Sever your head and shoulders from your body for a minute. Given that we are trying to get the attention up to your face, it's pretty important that the jewellery you adorn it with is right. Whether you are a silver or gold type of person, the same principles of verticals and horizontals apply.

* A long face can be balanced by rounder earrings that don't dangle from the lobe. Hoops must be kept small.

* A round face can be corrected with larger hoops, or longer chandelier-type earrings.

* A short neck can also be corrected with larger hoops, or longer chandelier-type earrings. Necklaces need to be no shorter than 6 centimetres below the clavicle (collarbone). Never, ever, ever wear a choker.

* A long neck can be balanced with a necklace that sits on the collarbone, or with a choker.

* You can wear statement earrings or a statement necklace, but you can't wear both. You will look like a Christmas tree.

* If you are wearing a statement ring or bracelet, make sure you get a manicure.

* If you wear seriously large bling, people will assume it's fake. Going smaller and taking care of your pieces so that they always sparkle will create an illusion that your bling is the real thing.

It's in the bag

While we are constantly exposed to the handbag of the minute and the shoe of the quarter hour, it's really important to realise that designers use celebrities as walking billboards. Choose the star you would like to be before rushing out and throwing the Visa down to get the accessory you have been told you need.

In general, tall people, like the Elle Macphersons of the world, can get away with bigger bags, Birkins, totes and hobos. Height is required to balance the strong handbag emphasis. Can someone please tell those Olsen girls?

A lavishly detailed handbag will make the area where it sits appear larger by default. This is why the choice of accessories is so important. All that hard work choosing the right clothing can be undone with one badly chosen handbag.

Shorter Kylie-sized people are better with styles like the saddle bag, the Fendi B bag and the Lanvin Pochette.

But, clutches work for everyone.

Whether it's a shoulder bag worn high or sitting low on the hip, a handbag worn over the elbow or carried in the hand, the placement and attention your accessory takes will have an impact.

The lowdown on accessories

Jewellery, belts and bags all have a role to play. **Statement colours, metallics and fancy trims should be considered with a Dot to Dot approach**. Your accessories can punctuate the outfit where required, or, if used incorrectly, can draw the eye towards your Worst Enemies. And think about the big picture. Have you gone too far? Are there too many highlight areas going on? If so, rethink your choices. Remember Coco Chanel's famous advice to take one thing off before leaving the house.

Killer Feature: legs galore

Aim for: longer pendants and beads, subdued earrings, bangles and bracelets, rings, low-sitting shoulder bags or handbags worn over the elbow, smaller statement bags that sit below the waist level.

With consideration, settle for: belts worn low, higher necklaces, high-sitting shoulder bags.

Avoid: waisted belts, statement earrings, larger totes and hobos.

Killer Feature: great hips and thighs

Aim for: longer pendants and beads, subdued earrings, bangles and bracelets, rings, low-sitting shoulder bags or handbags worn over the elbow, smaller statement bags that hit below the waist level.

With consideration, settle for: belts worn low.

Avoid: high-sitting shoulder bags, waisted belts, high necklaces and statement earrings.

Killer Feature: smaller waist

Aim for: feature belts, necklaces worn quite high, longer pendants and beads, smaller statement bags that hit the waist level or handbags worn over the elbow.

With consideration, settle for: clutches, bracelets, subdued earrings.

Avoid: large handbags, totes and hobos.

Killer Feature: great back

Aim for: earrings only, statement shoulder bags worn low, clutches can be stronger in colour or in sparkle factor.

With consideration, settle for: bracelets and rings.

Avoid: necklaces, feature belts.

Killer Feature: great bust

Aim for: necklaces that sit high, earrings with presence, but not huge ones, clutches should be darker, shoulder bags worn high can be brighter.

With consideration, settle for: arm bands worn high on the bicep, brooches.

Avoid: long necklaces, bangles, pendants that get lost in the cleavage, feature belts.

Killer Feature: great shoulders and neck

Aim for: statement earrings, clutches should be darker, shoulder bags worn high can be brighter.

With consideration, settle for: necklaces that sit high.

Avoid: long beads, bangles, feature belts.

Worst Enemy: short legs, longer torso

Aim for: higher necklaces and prominent earrings, high-sitting statement shoulder bags, smaller dark clutches.

With consideration, settle for: medium-length necklaces and statement beads.

Avoid: bracelets and bangles, rings, belts, large totes and hobos.

Worst Enemy: short torso

Aim for: statement earrings, high necklaces, low-sitting shoulder bags or handbags worn over the elbow, smaller statement bags that hit below the waist level. Totes and hobos are good.

With consideration, settle for: arm bands at the bicep.

Avoid: handbags that reach the elbow, longer necklaces and beads, belts.

Worst Enemy: chunky arms

Aim for: bracelets and rings, prominent earrings, low-sitting shoulder bags or handbags worn over the elbow, smaller statement bags that hit below the waist level. Totes and hobos are good.

With consideration, settle for: pendants that sit high.

Avoid: shoulder bags that sit high.

Worst Enemy: no waist

Aim for: statement earrings, either very high or quite low-sitting statement shoulder bags or handbags worn over the elbow falling at hip level.

With consideration, settle for: high necklaces.

Avoid: belts.

Worst Enemy: large hips

Aim for: statement earrings, high necklaces, high-sitting statement shoulder bags, darker clutch bags.

With consideration, settle for: statement beads and chunkier necklaces.

Avoid: belts, hobos and large totes.

Worst Enemy: large bust

Aim for: bracelets and rings, subdued earrings, low-sitting statement shoulder bags, brighter clutch bags.

With consideration, settle for: high necklaces.

Avoid: long beads and pendants, brooches, anything that gets lost in cleavage, belts, statement shoulder bags worn high.

Worst Enemy: broad shoulders

Aim for: bracelets and rings, subdued earrings, longer shaped earrings, low-sitting statement shoulder bags, brighter clutch bags.

With consideration, settle for: long beads and pendants, belts.

Avoid: statement shoulder bags worn high, totes and hobos.

Worst Enemy: short neck

Aim for: long beads and pendants, bangles, bracelets and rings, low-sitting statement shoulder bags, brighter clutch bags.

With consideration, settle for: brooches.

Avoid: high necklaces.

Star style: footwear

You need to know this.

* The most lengthening shoe you can wear is a nude-coloured, thin-sole high heel with a pointy toe.

* If your body is naturally a little thicker, so should your heel be. And chunky platforms should be given great consideration at all times.

* If you cannot guarantee that your feet are picture perfect, you just can't wear a shoe with an open heel and/or open toes. Get a pedicure or get enclosed shoes.

* The general rule is that shoes should tone in with your outfit, unless you are wearing black. This can be a little heavy and draw attention downwards.

* The best time of day to try potential new shoes on is the late afternoon as your feet will be slightly bigger than in the morning.

* While I love to buy new shoes as much as the next girl, remember that the attention is meant to move upwards towards the face. So if your shoes take up too much emphasis in the outfit, it's not good. It's sad, but true.

The lowdown on footwear

Killer Feature: great ankles

You can afford to: wear strappy shoes that wrap at the ankle. Mules and slides also work for you.

Look for: statement colours and textures if you like them. Embellishment at the ankle will work for you.

Boots: your best choice is a boot that stays close to the leg. Ankle boots that feature detail revealing your fine ankles are good.

Killer Feature: small feet

You can afford to: wear open-toed shoes and heavily embellished shoes. Metallics are also fine.

Look for: pointed toes or chisel toes in preference to round toes.

Boots: ankle boots can work as the area can get the balance it needs. Otherwise try fitted boots in preference to slouch boots.

Killer Feature: long legs

You can afford to: wear sparkle-arkle shoes, which will work on you.

Look for: statement colours and darker tones

Boots: if you really must do *Pretty Woman* you can. Otherwise, fitted to the knee will be best.

Worst Enemy: thick ankles

Avoid: chunky shoes, strappy shoes, Mary Janes and metallics.

Look for: classic pumps in subdued tones with no interruption to the line of the foot.

Boots: slouch boots will cover your problem.

Worst Enemy: big feet

Avoid: open-toed shoes, pointy-toed shoes.

Look for: enclosed pumps that are darker in tone with little embellishment. Ankle straps and Mary Janes will shorten the foot, which can be helpful. Look for a roundish toe or a chisel toe.

Boots: Long, lean boots are best.

Worst Enemy: short legs

Avoid: chunky shoes, dark shoes, strappy shoes, Mary Janes, and metallics.

Look for: nude-coloured high heels, pointy toes for length, paler tones generally.

Boots: tricky. Unless you can find ones that are shorter than the usual knee-high boots, I would advise you not to go there.

9

Star Scape
(the Look Book)

Dresses

Basic

These dresses all feature a slightly dropped waistline and thin belt, which are good for people with short torsos. The vertical tucks at the high hip add interest and would be used for people who have small hips.

◀ **Boat neck:** for narrow shoulders and people who have long necks as it introduces a strong horizontal through the neck, but offers no verticals.

▶**Rounded off square neckline:** introduces a bust horizontal and offers length through the neck and therefore is better for shorter necks and smaller busts. The short sleeves also help a smaller bust.

▶**Deep V neckline:** introduces more vertical for larger busts, and also for those with shorter necks.

A-line

These dresses feature different waist treatments, and are in an A-line shape which is good for hippier builds.

◄ **Deep round neckline:** introduces a bust horizontal and offers length through the neck and therefore is better for shorter necks and smaller busts. The short puff sleeves also help a smaller bust. The lack of waist seam offers length to a short torso.

► **Polo neck:** for broader shoulders and people who have long necks as it shortens the neck, offering no verticals. The high seam under the bust is good for longer torsos. The darker tone of skirt will help hide larger hips as will the A line shape.

◄ **V wrap neckline:** introduces verticals and diffuses larger busts, and helps those with shorter necks.

Party

These dresses all feature the use of gathers and ties, and a longer skirt shape finishing under the bust, which is good for people lacking waists or those with long bodies.

▶**Sweetheart:** for narrow shoulders and people who have shorter necks. The gathers and colour break introduces a strong horizontal through the bust, and the style offers verticals with straps and the dip to the centre of the bust. The darker tone skirt hides wider hips and the cascading drape gives a vertical through the body.

◀**Rounded off square neckline with gathers:** introduces a shoulder horizontal and offers width through that area with the contrast tie and bow. Better for smaller busts.

◀**Deep V neckline:** introduces verticals for a shorter neck or those with wider shoulders. The gathers are horizontals and create a fuller looking bust. The tie at the front offers verticals.

Gathered and draped detail

These dresses all feature gathered fabric used as a drape detail to maximise killer features.

◄ **Cross front:** to draw attention away from a fuller bust with the criss cross lines and define a smaller waist. Adds length to the neck.

►**Ruched strapless top:** adds bulk to bust and the darker skirt minimises the hips. Shows off good shoulders and a long neck.

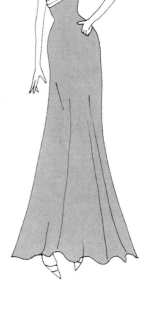

►**Halter drape:** minimises the waist and adds verticals through the bodice and lengthens the neck. The fuller skirt hides the hips.

Simple, clean lines

These dresses feature no detail; just clean lines to flatter the body.

◀ **Strapless with bolero:** the strong horizontal across the bust is given verticals with the jacket neckline. This adds length to the neck and perceived width to the bust.

▶ **Extended boat neck:** for narrow shoulders and people who have long necks as it introduces a strong horizontal through the neck, but offers no verticals. The high seam under the bust lengthens the body.

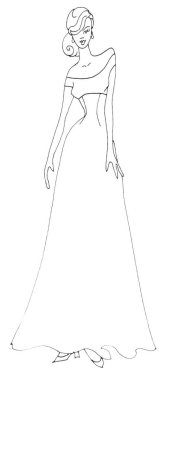

▶ **Rounded off square neckline:** introduces a bust horizontal and offers length through the neck and therefore is better for shorter necks. The curved under-bust seam encourages a smaller waist.

Tucks and drapes

These dresses all feature gathered fabric used as a drape detail to maximise killer features.

◀ **Cross front:** to draw attention away from a fuller bust with the diagonal drapes sending the eye north and south. The brooch detail highlights a small waist.

▶**Tucks in bust:** adds bulk to the bust and broadens the shoulders with the eye moving in a wide V direction. Shows off straight shoulders and lengthens the neck. The curved under-bust colour break makes the real waist smaller.

▶**Hip drape:** minimises the waist and plays up small hips. Good for a short torso. The drape skirt detail adds verticals and minimises the hips.

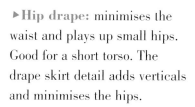

Athletic necklines

These dresses feature an athletic neckline, which is good to broaden the bust and show off straight shoulders.

◄ **With gathers:** to add little verticals at the bust area and give more perceived neck length. The colour break band at the hip highlights smaller hips or could be used on shorter torsos to create more length.

▶**With neck drape:** to add width at the shoulders with a draped colour break. The high under-bust seam gives a smaller waist as it is curved, and the mermaid shape skirt will work best on women with killer hips and thighs.

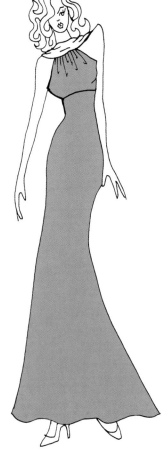

Colour breaks

These dresses use colour breaks to make the principle of light and dark work to reduce larger areas or highlight smaller ones. The knife neckline offers a slice of vertical to elongate the neck.

▶ **Puff sleeves:** and a pale bodice for narrow shoulders and small busts. The dark tone skirt hides wide hips and is better for a long torso or for those lacking waist definition.

◀ **Sleeveless:** is better for wide shoulders and a lower finishing bodice is good for those with short torsos. A darker skirt hides large hips.

◀ **One block tone:** with a strong slice of contrast through the skirt offers a good vertical aspect. The break under the bust is good for long bodies.

Skirts

◄ **The A line skirt:** flatters wide hips and thighs as the general direction of the shape glides over them. A facing, rather than a waistband, makes a smooth finishing point to the skirt and works well under unforgiving knits.

► **The straight skirt:** sits at the true waist and is better suited to slim hips and thighs. Again, a simplified area at the waist makes it smooth and more flattering unless you can afford to carry embellishment there.

► **The high waisted tulip skirt:** is for those with small waists as there is so much focus in that area. The downwards sloping pockets give some balance to the height of the waistband.

◄ **The tiered skirt:** was made for tall people who can actually afford to lose the 5 centimentres of height per horizontal break. It does hide wide hips and thighs though, so if you are tall and wide down below, consider it as an option.

►**A centre front placket:** with buttons creates a strong vertical through this A line skirt. The buttoned pocket tabs could be considered by those with a small waist, otherwise keep it simple.

Trousers

These styles play with the line to flatter specific body shapes.

◄ **True waist slouch:** broad hips and/or thighs are better in this style. The downwards sloping pockets diminish a wide bottom.

► **High-waisted palazzo:** the high waist is better for people who have long torsos. The very wide palazzo leg will disguise larger thighs.

► **Hip-detailed slim-line:** just below true waist, this style balances a short torso. The detail at the high hip highlights small hips.

▶**Capri:** good for short torsos with downwards sloping
pockets to flatter the hips.

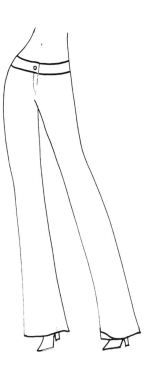

◀**True waist flare:** better on
small hips and thighs, it can
introduce some curves into the
picture if you are lacking waist
definition or are too skinny.
Also good for long torsos.

▶**Hipster straight leg:** the low
waist is better for short torsos,
and this simple classic leg
shape suits a great many
women, as long as the thigh area
is not too tight.

Jackets

For small shoulders

These jackets show how length can be used and what to look for with buttoning.

◀ **Cropped:** a strong line of three contrast buttons acts as a ladder. The three quarter sleeve highlights small hips and waist. A good choice for a short torso as the style validates it. The high neckline with thick feature band detail suits narrow shoulders.

▶**Low buttoning longer jacket:** introduces a strong vertical to mitigate a full bust. Upwards pointing lapels increase the shoulder width. Angled welt pockets take the eye to a perceived small waist. The longer line is better to conceal a full hip.

▶**Wide two-button neckline:** introduces strong chest horizontals which is good for a small bust and also uses gathers at the sleeve head to increase the bust and shoulder area. The short length is good for small hips or to mitigate a long torso.

For broad shoulders

▶ **Cropped:** a deep V neckline takes the eye in a vertical sweep away from the shoulders. The feature button acts as a diversion to the eye and the swing shape with three quarter sleeve highlights small hips and waist. A good choice for a short body with broad shoulders.

◀ **Low buttoning longer jacket:** introduces a strong vertical to mitigate a full bust. Downwards facing lapels are better for wider shoulders. Straight pocket tabs and the long line play down a full hip.

▶ **Shawl neckline:** introduces strong chest verticals; good for a large bust. The raglan sleeves, which are set in on a diagonal line, diminish broad shoulders.

Sleeves

The length of sleeve and any fullness in its shape has a flow-on effect on other parts of the body.

◄ **Fitted sleeve:** finishing just below the elbow is a flattering length as it elongates the arms.

►**Lantern:** to take the eye away from a broad shoulder. Good for killer hips or waists, as the fullness sits there.

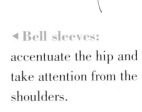

◄ **Bell sleeves:** accentuate the hip and take attention from the shoulders.

◄**Tulip sleeves:** good for slim hips and waists as the sleeve fullness hits that area.

►**Leg o'mutton:** fullness at the shoulder increases this area and also has an impact on the bust, which will seem bigger.

Necklines

To broaden shoulders

These necklines draw the eye horizontally but the variations of line can play up killer features, too. You can also add perceived mass to the bust and diminish the waist by widening the shoulders.

◄ **Boat neck:** this is a clean neckline that sweeps high across the collarbone.

▶ **Squared off boat neck:** adds a little more to neck length, but similar in effect to the classic boat neck.

▶ **High rounded off square:** better than a rounded scoop neck as it gives width to the shoulders.

▶ **Lower rounded off square:** a very flattering neckline as it gives length through the neck, and is one to use if you are also emphasising the bust.

◄ **Extended boat neck:** a retro favourite, this one sits slightly off the shoulders and is a good alternative to strapless if you are narrow through the shoulders.

To slim shoulders

Keep the cut close to the neck if you want to diminish the shoulder area, and go for styles which add length from chin to bust.

▶**Classic round neck:** this simple neckline works best with more depth to give a stronger vertical.

◀**Inverted triangle:** like the low rounded off square neckline, this is very flattering and gives a great line to smaller busts. It needs to start quite close to the neck to work best.

▶**Knife:** this slice of skin from chin to bust adds lots of vertical.

◀**Sweetheart:** a blend of the knife and the inverted triangle, it relies on starting close to the neck to work best, giving maximum vertical impact.

Cowl

These draped necklines move the eye in specific directions and can play up a killer bust.

▶**Deep cowl:** this needs to start close to the neck and will lengthen the area between chin and bust, as well as taking the emphasis off broad shoulders.

◀**Wide cowl:** broadens the shoulders and emphasises the bust.

▶**High funnel-neck cowl:** an alternative to the athletic neckline, but can be problematic for those with short necks.

Strapless

These necklines all draw the eye horizontally to broaden narrow shoulders. You add perceived mass to the bust and diminish the waist by widening the shoulders.

◄ **Sweetheart or bow shape:** the one strapless style that diminishes broad shoulders, it also creates neck length with the centre drop in the bust.

► **Straight across:** creates a strong line across the bust.

◄ **Curved towards face:** better for those with long necks and good for defining a strong bust horizontal.

► **Curved towards waist:** better to elongate the neck as there is a deeper drop to the centre of the neckline.

Bikini

This neckline moves the eye to play up a killer bust. The strap separation has an effect on the design too.

▶**Wide separation:** the wide line created here will broaden the shoulders and make the waist seem smaller.

◀**Close separation:** makes the neck seem longer but can make the waist seem larger. Better for empire line dresses and baby dolls where the waist is hidden.

▶**Halter:** this cut elongates the neck, defines the waist and makes a strong line across the bust.

Wedding dresses

Slimline

The high under-bust seam on four of these designs will flatter many, as the garment detail is close to the face.

◄ **Cap sleeves:** take attention off broader shoulders, which are also helped by the deep V neckline meeting a curved under-bust seam with detail. The A line skirt flatters wider thighs.

▶**For a smaller waist**, the pleated detail is good to elongate the neck and highlight the centre of the body. The A line skirt, again, is great for wider thighs.

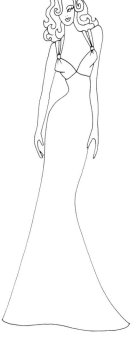

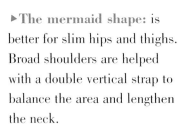

▶**The mermaid shape:** is better for slim hips and thighs. Broad shoulders are helped with a double vertical strap to balance the area and lengthen the neck.

▶**A beaded:** rounded off square neckline with an upwardly curving under-bust seam keeps the eye on a killer bust and shoulder area, and adds length to the neck. Again, the mermaid skirt is a good option for slim thighs and hips, but go for an A line shape if your thighs are wide.

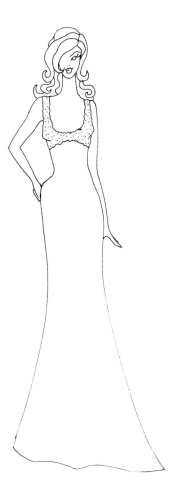

◀**Wide feature straps:** give narrow shoulders more width, while the inverted V under-bust seam with embellishment draws attention towards the face.

Full skirt

These designs could all be adapted to full meringue if you really must be the princess bride. They flatter those with serious hip and thigh issues. A full veil will work well with these gowns as it balances with the skirt shapes.

◄ **A lower than true waist:** will flatter short torsos, while the embellished drape at the bust gives more volume to that area and continues with the dropped straps across the biceps.

▶ **A small waist:** is needed to make the horizontal detail work at the midriff. Beaded lace enhances a killer bust and the strong vertical folds give an upwards lift to the design.

▶**The strapless bodice:** is ruched vertically which builds a small bust. Under-bust embellishment takes attention away from full hips which are hidden under the princess line skirt.

◀**Inverted pleats:** create good verticals through this princess line gown. The embellishment across the shoulders broadens the area while the deeply scooped neckline adds length to the neck. Three quarter length sleeves with detail at the ends are slimming to large arms.

Take Me
to the Stars

The Wardrobe Mistress's kit

Here I focus on cheating, fixing and manipulation. Sounds like an episode of *The Bold and the Beautiful*, but it's what a Wardrobe Mistress does to get things over the line.

I have a number of tricks in my standby bag that every good television stylist should know about, and a number of basic essentials that I *always* have on hand so I can rescue any wardrobe malfunction.

I have listed them in no particular order.

Tapeits by The Useful Chick Stuff Company

Yes, I do use double-sided tape. I firmly believe a gown should fit you properly and the tape is just used for malfunctions. It should never be the basis of choosing a dress. If a dress doesn't look right without tape DON'T BUY IT.

The natural enemy of Tapeits is the spray tan. Unless the tan has been under the shower after the 12-hour mark has elapsed, you are going to have trouble. The tape will not stick.

The other natural enemies of Tapeits are body moisturizer and body shimmer. So, if you absolutely must use them please remember where you intend to apply tape.

The friend of Tapeits is witch hazel. In a pinch, you can apply some with a cotton ball to remove the moisturizer/shimmer/spray tan from the small area to be taped.

Witch hazel, available at chemists is a clear astringent which will save you from anything and everything. It is less than £3 for a bottle that will last ages, and will remove moisturizer, as mentioned above, take the itch out of insect bites, clear blemishes, even remove gummy marks from sticker residue on shoes etc.

Liftits by The Useful Chick Stuff Company

Oh, these really are about the best thing since the Wonder Bra. They will lift up the saggiest, most pendulous breasts and make them all pert and pretty again. If you have enormous bosoms, you can use two sets. And if you have a smaller bust, they are great for the dresses you can't wear a bra with, for example a backless dress, but would like a little support. They are tricky to get your head around as they support from above the nipple, not below. Take my advice and try them out before the big day with a practice run. Sober, please. Very discreet and fabulous.

As with Tapeits, their natural enemies are spray tan, moisturizer and shimmer.

Concealits by The Useful Chick Stuff Company

Brilliant for covering smuggled peanuts. Use two sets if you are really anxious about this.

As with Tapeits, their natural enemies are spray tan, moisturizer and shimmer. Is this sinking in yet? I have a problem with shimmer and spray tans.

Boostits by The Useful Chick Stuff Company

How we love fakery! Boostits are not the only silicone inserts out there but they are the ones I like the best. They quickly transform a small-busted girl into a vixen. But make sure any fittings you have for your dress are done with the Boostits in place, as they add a good 4cm to the bust measurement.

Fluffies

These were the solution before God made silicone. They are little round discs of foam, available at haberdashery stores. A bit like foam party hats really. I like to fold them in half and sew them into the bottom of the bra cups of corsets to add volume under the bust. Or you can sew them into strapless dresses which tend to flatten a bust. They let your natural bust sit on top and look nice and fleshy. And I prefer them to chicken fillets because they will not fall out on the dance floor if you work up a sweat. And really, I am over that embarrassing moment of 1998. Really I am.

Press studs

I like to buy big press studs and sew them onto the top edge of a corset that is going under a gown. Particularly a strapless gown. Having the dress attached to the corset means that you don't have to worry about whether the dress and the corset have parted ways during the evening. Even if you drink yourself under the table quite literally, your dress and corset will not have parted ways. You can safely wave goodbye to your guests without the flash of corsetry under the arms too.

Bra strap keepers

You can buy these in haberdashery stores and online. They are sewn into centre of dress straps and have little popper studs in which to catch the bra straps. They keep everything together and offer a little more security. At a pinch you can use safety pins, but make sure that the bra strap can move freely inside the pin, rather than piercing the strap with the pin. This means you will avoid the telltale mark where the pin is positioned.

Leukopore tape

This is a surgical tape from the chemist which looks like Magic tape in that it is clear. It is very adhesive and is great for taping bra straps into linings, or securing brooch pins inside the lining of the garment etc. You can also use it inside hats to stop make-up getting on the band lining and just peel it off later.

Leukoplast tape

Another surgical tape, this sturdier flesh-coloured one is handy if you are using a stick-on bra to give it extra security under the bust. Check and recheck the tape is not visible when you are dressed.

Packing tape

This tape is super sticky and my favourite for defluffing dark garments. It picks up everything from cat hair to cookie crumbs.

Scholl Party Feet Gel Cushions by The Useful Chick Stuff Company

Made especially for the Dancing Party Posse, these gel cushions are so good when you are going to be in killer heels all night. They are washable and reusable, which is a bonus.

Shoe repair shop

While we are down there with your feet, please consider this. Having your shoes stretched across the widest part of your foot will make a lot of difference when your little tootsies start to swell under the pressure of being tortured all night. I do it with every pair I own.

Scholl Party Feet Heel Shields by The Useful Chick Stuff Company

I often find that clients slip out of their shoes if they have narrow feet, so heel grips are my saviours. I also use Tapeits under the heel to secure their feet into precarious shoes, just in case.

Scholl Party Feet Heel Cushions by The Useful Chick Stuff Company

These are similar to the larger gel cushions for underneath the ball of the feet, except these gel cushions that sit under the heel for extra comfort.

Hairspray

Avoid slipping in your new shoes by spraying them and leaving them to sit for a few minutes to get tacky. It's an old dance-school trick.

Scholl Party Feet Slingback Strips by The Useful Chick Stuff Company

These latex strips keep your slingbacks from slipping and also protect the heels from blisters.

Commando supplies

If you are going commando for the sake of the frock remember the age-old starlet's secret. A tampon. Enough said.

White chalk

In the event that somehow you get a mark on your wedding frock, chalk over it and blot it with a tissue. It won't disappear but it will be much less visible.

Baby powder

Another good one for brides, especially if you know the mark is oil based. Baby powder soaks up the oil very well and then you just need to brush it off.

Saliva

This is really weird, but I swear it's true. If you get blood on silk (only silk) have the person who owns the blood spit on the stain and rub gently with a cloth and it will go. I don't know why this works. But it does.

Cornflour

If you get an oil mark on leather, sprinkle liberally with cornflour and let it rest a minute. Dust it off and repeat the process, but rather than dusting it off the second time, rub it like crazy building up lots of friction (i.e. heat) and the mark will be much less visible.

Dry-cleaning fluid

Having a little bottle of this is handy for those marks that appear out of nowhere. The faster you act upon a stain, the better your chances of removing it. I do warn you though to patch test it on a part of the garment that is not obvious, like the inside of the hem or seam allowance, in case there is a dodgy reaction.

Wet Ones

The less fumey version of dry-cleaning fluid. But not always as effective.

Anti-static spray

Essential kit requirement. If you have none, in a pinch you can use hairspray or water spray on the lining only. Or rub moisturizer on your legs as I find it the most effective remedy for static.

Pins

Get a little tin and fill it with very small gold safety pins, very small black safety pins (annoyingly blunt, I must say, but less visible than gold in a darker garment), larger silver safety pins and flat dressmaking pins. Wherever possible, use dressmaking pins when you are trying to conceal something as they are much flatter and therefore less visible. But if you are pinning something that is under pressure or strain, use a safety pin. You can work it out, I'm sure.

Needle and thread

Here's a no-brainer. Have sharp scissors and a needle and thread that matches your dress on standby just in case. You can't imagine how easily you can avert disaster the old-fashioned way.

Just in case:

* A seam splits.

* The zip gets stuck or broken. A Marilyn Monroe moment.

* The hem comes down.

* A strap breaks.

* Also good for sewing a brooch onto a frock that has sentimental value to ensure it really, really, really can't fall off and be lost forever.

You get the idea.

Having a well-stocked kit like this ready to roll will prevent any wardrobe malfunction from ruining your day.

Star sites

The following is a list of the Wardrobe Mistress's essential items, brands and their websites.

Allure Lingerie www.allurelingerie.co.uk

The Useful Chick Stuff Company www.usefulchickstuff.co.uk

Debenhams www.debenhams.com

Intimate Attitudes www.lingerieexpress.co.uk

Lingerie Express www.lingerieexpress.co.uk

Lady Grace www.ladygrace.com

Lauren Silva www.laurensilva.com

Naomi and Nicole www.tempestra.co.uk

Annette www.figleaves.com

Body Wrap www.figleaves.com

Wacoal www.figleaves.com

Huit Lingerie www.figleaves.com

Doreen Fashions www.doreenfashions.com

Elle MacPherson www.zodee.co.uk

Miraclesuit www.rigbyandpeller.com

Figleaves www.figleaves.com

Victoria's Secret www.victoriassecret.com

Fayreform www.twenga.co.uk

Vogue Patterns Online www.voguepatterns.com

Fine Lines Lingerie www.zodee.co.uk

Zodee www.zodee.co.uk

Glamour Corsets www.glamourcorsets.com.au

Nancy Ganz www.zodee.co.uk

Loveable www.zodee.co.uk

The U Bra www.figleaves.com

STAR SAVERS

It never ceases to amaze me how many people cannot sew. At all. And that's just the stylists working in the fashion industry.

Here are some absolute no-brainers so that you don't have to take everything to the alterations lady down the road . . .

Repairing a hem

1 Press the hem crease into place with an iron so that your fabric is even.
2 Using dressmaker's pins, at 90-degree angles to the hem, pin the hem up at 6 centimetre intervals. (Work from the inside of the garment and you will be less likely to make mistakes.) Have the inside edge of the garment facing you.
3 Thread your needle with about 45 centimetres' length and tie a decent knot at one end, allowing 15 centimetres of the other end to fall through the eye and dangle freely.
4 Make your first stitch at a seam join and pull the thread right up to the knot.
5 Take the needle through a little of the turn-up edge, then, coming back towards your body, take one tiny stitch from the actual garment. Take another stitch from the turn-up edge, still moving back towards your body, then another from the garment.

Remember, all the time you are sewing towards your body.
Make sure you keep the thread quite loose as you sew, in order
to keep the hem from looking tight.

6 At the end of the hem, make another tiny stitch into the seam
join and then tuck the needle back into that stitch to make a
good knot. Cut off the excess thread and press the hem again.

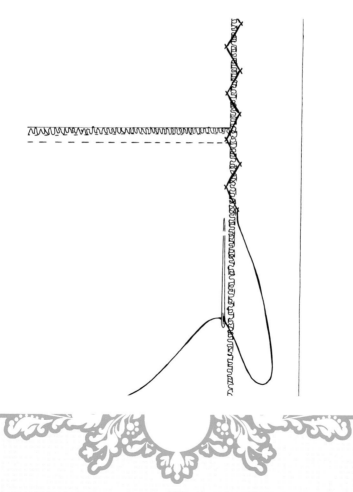

197

Replacing a button

1 Thread your needle with a double strand and make a decent knot at the end.
2 Position the button where it needs to go and, starting at the reverse of the fabric, push the needle right through and out the first hole in the button.
3 Sew down into the next hole, through to the back of the garment again. Keep the button a little loose as you go.

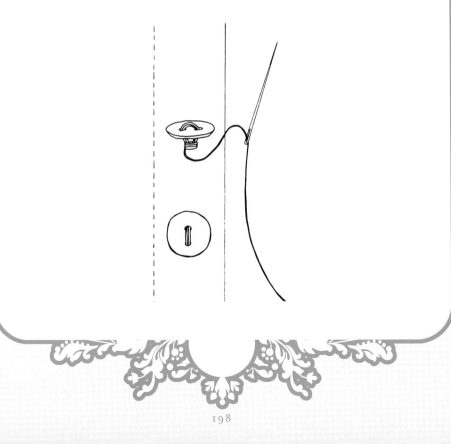

4 Continue two more times to the front of the button and back to the reverse side.
5 Push the needle up through to the outside of the fabric, but not through the actual button this time.
6 Wind the thread around the base of the button, enclosing the stitches and creating a shank, then push the needle back to the reverse side.
7 Make a tiny stitch and a knot, then cut the excess thread away.

Stuck zipper?

Try rubbing a cake of soap along the zipper teeth and easing the zip head out of its position.

Lucky Stars

The inside story

Introduction

I created this favourite gown for my favourite contestant on the first season of Australia's *The Biggest Loser*, Fiona Faulkiner. She was likely to be a very photographable guest at the Logies, a TV industry event much like the National Television Awards. I decided that, based upon her star quality, Fiona needed to look extra fabulous and started a dress for her based only on what I could see on television as we had never met. The wardrobe girls at our Melbourne studios measured her for me after a publicity shoot and emailed me Fiona's specifics. Confused by how tall she would need to be to meet these measurements, I made the gown with the thought in the back of my mind that if she didn't like the dress or if it didn't fit, I could always rework it and wear it to my 40th birthday party later that year. Fiona's shape was basically mine with much, much longer legs. She did like the dress and it did fit. Perfectly. And we met finally on the afternoon of the awards when I dressed her. The gown was made from ombre silk georgette in Tequila sunrise hues, trimmed with antique Indian braid, which I beaded after application. My daughter Valentina, a very talented little jeweller, made some amazing earrings for Fiona to wear as well, featuring large teardrop Swarovski crystals and Czech re-cut crystals.

Chapter 1

This gown was the first of many that I made for my wonderful friend and serious Australian A-lister, Jessica Rowe. Shortly after moving from Melbourne, when I was still quite the new girl at the television studios in Sydney I suggested to Jessica that I would love to make her something special for the television awards of 2001. I half-expected that she would decline the offer, as Jess had so many designers who loved to dress her. But she was very excited at the idea. That first frock made from a heavily beaded silk chiffon sari purchased at the oh-so-wrong end of King Street, Newtown, a trendy but somewhat lowbrow inner suburb of Sydney, started a fabulous synergy that still bubbles away today. I had no idea when I found that gold sari of exactly what it wanted to be, but after draping it on the dressmaking stand and playing with it for a while, the design became clear. This one is a sentimental favourite of mine.

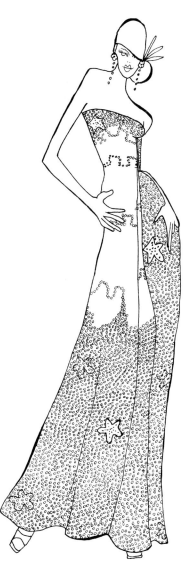

Chapter 2

I decided to call this 2003 ensemble
Daisy Does Derby after Daisy Buchanan
in *The Great Gatsby*. The fabric and
trims for this 1920s-inspired creation
were from a funny little haberdashery
store in Sydney's ragtrade district of
Surry Hills. The beaded appliqués that
were sewn onto the bust and the belt
were the start of the outfit. Again, it was
from the beautiful beading that the
design sprung because I had absolutely
no idea what I was going to make my
frock buddy Jessica for this important
racing outing. Derby Day is the first day
of Melbourne's Spring Racing Carnival,
a massive fashion event that culminates
in the Melbourne Cup on the first
Tuesday of November. I always laugh at
loud when I see this outfit because of its
history. At the time I was slaving away as
the key stylist for *Australian Idol*'s first
series and had become aware, the hard
way, of what years of wardrobe work can
do to a girl's back. Much of the hand
sewing on Jessica's outfit had been done
lying on my back in bed, with my arms
raised in the air and various heat packs,
painkillers and cushions supporting me.
I was determined to finish the outfit, see
our version of *Pop Idol* through to the
grand finale, and then have a few weeks
off …

Chapter 3

This one is called Audrey Goes To
Shanghai. It was another racing
ensemble I made, in a red silk
Chinese brocade with layers of
lace-trimmed tulle underneath. I
love the retro aspect to this frock
and the fact that I was praised for
adding the then very underused
fascinator to the look. It was made
in 2001, the time of brims, brims
and more brims so our little
ostrich-feather-trimmed whimsy
was quite the talking point at
Melbourne's Spring Racing
Carnival.

Chapter 4

Called a Kennedy Flemington, the beaded 1960s collar piece for this frock came from my favourite charity shop in Sydney's inner west. It's a top-secret destination. I purchased it many months before Derby Day 2004 was on the agenda and let it sit on my desk until it told me what it wanted to be. Again, I was incredibly busy with running the *Australian Idol* style team as Melbourne's Spring Racing Carnival was approaching, but I was determined to make this frock as well as starting another sparkly number I was thinking about: the winner of *Australian Idol*'s ornate ensemble for the audience of four million eager viewers of the Sydney Opera House grand finale. It was quite a month! My mother had also had an operation to remove a tumour at that time, so introspective and focused hand sewing was certainly a welcome distraction from the escalating chaos of that intense period. When the beading at the hip area of the racing dress took me late into the night at home, my husband Martyn sat up late and sewed with me. And two weeks later he would help me bead the winner's gown as well. You have to love a man that can sew!

Chapter 5

The television awards night of 2005 was shortly after the funeral of Pope John Paul II. I couldn't help but acknowledge as I sat up watching the funeral while hand sewing that the little Catholic girl inside me had been heavily influenced by her upbringing. Gold, ruby red and luxe fabrics everywhere. And just what I was working on too. There was more embellishment at that funeral than at any Oscars red carpet I have ever seen. The key gown I was making that year had a gold lamé underlay beneath the draped remnants of beaded sari tulle, heavily embellished on top. The lower part of the gown was cut from a silk burnout velvet I had found in a remnants bin at one of my favourite silk suppliers. It had damage, in the way of small holes, scattered throughout the bolt of fabric. I decided to chance it, as the design was so lovely and I had the ten metres I purchased dyed from pale pink to crimson. I cut around the damage very carefully and positioned the draping over an inner sheath, cut from a heavy silk satin in the best colour ever, chilli. This gown is one that I am very proud of.

Chapter 6

My second wedding dress is my favourite wedding dress. My second husband is also my favourite. Another trip to the sari Mecca, Campsie in Sydney's dodgy south west, found me purchasing a wonderful piece that was tulle based, variegating from cream to aubergine at the hem. It was heavily embellished in gold and silver sequins, but I would add many more crystals to the gown before it was finished. I did seven calico toiles, or tryouts really, of the dress before cutting the silk. To get the bodice to sit flat against the skin, I added an inner slip that was weighted with lead to pull it down firmly. My wedding dress took the whole summer to make and weighed 10kg after the lead addition, and I had welts in my shoulders at the end of that hysterically wet March day from the straps carrying the weight. So, it was officially my very last wedding dress ... I think!

Chapter 7

Way back in 1988 when the recession we Australians were told by our Prime Minister we "had to have" was settling in for a very long stay, my dear friend and colleague Maida Jereb and I decided we would start a lingerie label. Devetu was badly timed, as accessories were the first to feel the pain of the recession, but we made some wonderful pieces that were a breath of fresh air in a lingerie landscape that revolved around boring old lace and nylon. We did tartans, polka dots and Liberty-style prints in beautiful cottons. There was little well-made feminine cotton lingerie available at that time, and what you could find came from Italy and was very expensive. I look around now at the choices from low-end retailers to our finest lingerie boutiques and marvel at how good we have it. Boring lace and nylon lingerie is only a small part of the options these days. Thank heavens.

Chapter 8

When I decided to take company with me to the seriously unglamorous Indian shop in Newtown that day in 2002, I knew my client was in for an education. The store owner was only likely to take a sari down from its elevated hanger if you were definitely going to purchase it. Even then, after he brought it down from the hook, trying to look beyond the layers of dust and moth holes and see the potential in a piece of silk was a stretch. We were looking for a strong colour, and found it in the turquoise georgette sari embellished with silver and gold sequins. This gown was called The Hanging Gardens of Babylon, because of the floral appliqué detail that continued over the shoulder. Each flower was cut from the sari and backed with stable silk, then positioned on a second band of silk for strength. There was lead weighting in the hem to create the strong drape. Thanks to yet another hand-sewing marathon, this frock got lots of media attention, and it is one I still love today.

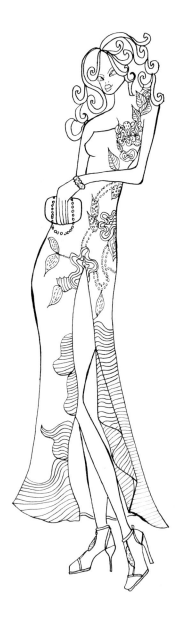

Chapter 9

Any stylist will tell you that the red carpet is a very competitive environment. The main objective of people like me behind the scenes is to present the press with something different from the hundreds of other gowns paraded, hoping for a place in the best-dressed pages. In 2006, I felt quite a strong and challenging silhouette was needed, a distraction from the sexy, draped gowns that I knew would flood the red carpet. I had made this client's wedding gown the year before so I knew her shape would work in a cinched-in style. We went for an aubergine heavy satin dress made from a vintage 1950s pattern. It featured a low sweeping strapless neckline and the style highlighted her tiny waist with a thick black band. I dread to remember how many metres of black tulle were in the petticoats underneath. Enough that she was concerned about being able to sit at the table for the duration of the event. The final touch was some wonderful retro make-up which brought out the Grace Kelly in her.

Chapter 10

This little number was called Carmen Loves to Tango. My friend and client Jessica wore it to Melbourne's Spring Racing Carnival in 2004. The bodice was made from a gorgeous fringed silk flamenco shawl purchased from my daughter's Spanish dancing school. I made a basic satin padded bustier with a side-separating zipper and draped the shawl onto it, catching it here and there, repositioning the floral embroidery where necessary. For something that was meant to look randomly draped around the body it certainly took a lot of time to get right. The skirt, a tiered satin flamenco-inspired piece, was made from the same green satin as the handbag I made for her. The shoes, which were handmade by one of the last masters of this profession in Australia, were also cut from this silk.

THE MERE MORTAL MANIFESTO

Tips

#1 Know your Worst Enemies.

#2 Know your One Killer Feature.

#3 People have lazy eyes.

#4 Always aim to keep the eye travelling upwards.

#5 Apply the Dot to Dot principle.

#6 The party shouldn't be downstairs.

#7 The lazy eye gets distracted easily.

#8 The lazy eye sees things in a simplistic way: wide area of body; less wide area of body.

#9 The simpler the waist area, the more flattering the design.

#10 The frock rocks.

Racing Rules

#1 Think of the hat as embellishment, physically removed from your clothing.

#2 Your feet are less than second fiddle.

#3 Hat size and colour are used to balance face shape.

#4 Simplify your jewellery.

#5 Make your makeup work.